FRANKLIN, OHIO 45005-2225

# *Men Are No Damn Good!*

## (pending further research)

Essays on Becoming a Man
by EUGENE J. WEBB

Cartoons by C. P. Houston

Resource Publications, Inc.
San Jose, California

Previous works by the author
*My Grandma Once Said*
*Life and Death of a Marriage*
*It's Not Easy Being Human*
*Lord, You Must Be Joking!*

Editorial director: Kenneth Guentert
Managing editor: Elizabeth J. Asborno
Copyeditor: Cathe Reed

© 1996 Resource Publications, Inc. All rights reserved. No part of this
work may be reprinted without permission from the publisher. For reprint
permission, write to:

Reprint Department
Resource Publications, Inc.
160 E. Virginia Street #290
San Jose, CA 9512-5876

**Library of Congress Cataloging in Publication Data**
Webb, Eugene J., 1940-
    Men are no damn good (pending further research) : essays on
  becoming a man / Eugene J. Webb.
     p.      cm.
   ISBN 0-89390-343-4 (pbk.)
   1. Men—Humor. 2. Men—Conduct of life—Humor. I. Title.
  PN6231.M45W43   1996
  814'.54—dc20                              95-33679

Printed in Canada

00 99 98 97 96 | 5 4 3 2 1

To Joshua D. Webb,
who taught our family
that being a man is not about age
or knowledge or power or accomplishments.
It is about loving and being loved,
taking charge of one's brief life,
trusting the necessity of pain,
and leaving when it is time.

# Contents

# Acknowledgments

Thank you, Marty, my wife and my friend, for your brilliant technical assistance, critical reviews, and moral support in this work. Together we made it happen.

Thank you, Jean, Justin, and John, for your excellent and humorous editing of the manuscript. I'm surrounded by geniuses.

Thank you, Maria and Goly and all the other attentive waitresses of André's, Avalon Drug, and House of Pies, who served my hot coffee as I wrote and who laughed in agreement with the book's title.

Thank you, Resource Publications, Inc., for your openness to producing this work and to promoting its success.

And, finally, thank you, all the men and women in my life who have played a part in my awakening to the beauty and complexity of human nature.

# Disclaimer

This is *not* a self-help book. We men don't need help. And you gals know by now that you're wasting your time slipping this or any book under our coffee cups or stuck behind our toothbrushes. We know what you're doing. It won't work.

This book is about men becoming men, *not* about women "coping" with men, nor even about how to better appreciate or love men. We guys are quite lovable already, thank you. We may not be easy to live with, but we are lovable.

This book is for pure pleasure. We guys need to laugh at ourselves, brag about ourselves, and cry about ourselves. We need to do our own growing up, our own waking up—when we're ready (whatever that means!).

So if you, the reader, man or woman, find in this book some brilliant insights into the male mind, some incredibly helpful piece to your life puzzle, or some unnerving wisdom about yourself or your man, then know in advance that your discoveries were totally unintended by the author.

If after thirty pages you are not enjoying yourself, throw the darn thing away!

Eugene J. Webb

# Introduction: "Men Are No Damn Good!"

Somebody had to say it. Heaven knows that enough men walk the plank of silent doubt, whispering, "What's *wrong* with me?" Heaven knows that enough women share in the secret recesses of ladies' rooms, "What's wrong with men, anyhow?" It has fallen upon me to finally answer this age-old question.

The more popular answer to the question of what is wrong with men echoed by women far and wide is: Men are no damn good. The well-documented, scientific response is: Men are no damn good. Pending further research, of course. Fifty million women and fifty million case examples can't be wrong. Besides, my mother can't be wrong, and she was the first one to inform me of this profound truth.

Sure, sure. Lots of people say that they have heard of exceptions, or that there were good ones for a brief period of time, or that a book or a movie has hinted at a really wonderful man. We've all heard the rumors. But if you dig far enough into those encrusted masculine layers of mind, body, and spirit, what do you find? Disappearance, mutism, trout-addiction, success mania, mowing obsession, beer, toys, wealth, and sex. Cripples, every one!

Men are not what they say they are. They live multiple lives. They take control of almost everything under the sun, from business to politics, finance to fashion, environment to education. Then when things turn to rack and ruin, they scream it's not their fault, that they were misunderstood, that if they had more—yes, more—support from women, then they.... Oh, my God! I mean *we*! I'm one of them. What am I doing!?

"Yes, what are you doing?" asked Marty, my wife and chief critic, as she handed back to me the rough draft of this book.

"Trying to make a name for yourself by bashing men? Eager to instill even more despair in the hearts of us women who know all too well the frustration of standing by our men in loneliness and bewilderment and self-blame? You want me, a woman, to help you, a man, publish this, this wonderfully humorous and stingingly sober look at the operational mind and heart of men today?"

It was one of those moments that every man dreads: having to admit his dependence on a woman's expertise to get a man's job done, only later to diminish her significance by including her name in the ever-so-brief acknowledgment page of the book of our lives. I asked her help. Marty agreed. But she demanded more than a byline. She wanted her cut of the royalties. I acquiesced. She accepted. I pouted. She gloated. I couldn't tell if I had won or she had won.

"*We* won," I remember her saying, although I still have no idea what that means.

I remember once reading a book entitled *It's Not Easy Being Human*. I think the author could have said that it's not easy being a man. We guys hope no one ever asks us, "Hey, bud, what's it like being a man?" We hope to stay busy enough that we never have to wonder about it. We hope that we die before being found out. We hope that our secret lives are never written about in an entertaining and challenging book, because then we might want to read it.

Men don't do psychology; women do psychology. Men don't change; women change. Men fight their whole lives to remain hidden; it's women who want to share their kidneys, their worries, and their dreams. We men know that whatever we expose, we will be held accountable for, and it will later be held against us. Women expose everything and defend nothing. We're not the same. Mother Nature, in her infinite humor, made us that way, so no rib-tickling book is going to get us guys to be different from what we've always been: brats!

So there. Enough said. The contents of this book are strictly for entertainment purposes, not for the suspected hidden purpose of stirring insight, provocation, or a challenge for men to grow the hell up.

# Who Was That Masked Man?

*Forethought*   What are little boys made of? Not nails and snails and
puppy dog tails, although these are some of our
earliest toys. We little guys were made of teams and
dreams and heroic schemes. We wanted to be like
the men (and some women) we admired in sports, in
movies, in stories we read, and in dramas we heard.
We practiced how they walked and talked, how they
dressed, how they stood up to the world and stood
for something wonderful. These giants of our imagination would be with us forever.

Someday, much later, we would also acknowledge
the admirable qualities of our parents, brothers, and
sisters. But for these golden years of youth, our
hearts were set on those who opened our minds to
the finest of human ideals and the mysteries of life.

Out of the magical Wild West he rode, right into our living
rooms on Friday nights. Always a crisis—cattle rustlers,
ranch thieving, fights over water rights, stagecoach robbers,
the struggle of the homeless settlers and the unsettled
homesteaders. Each radio show captured our hearts as this
masked defender of justice and his trusted Native American

accomplice did their good work while we, the audience, were solely privileged to know his identity.

What a secret! What an honor! The hero is unidentified by victim and villain alike. He moves about without ever allowing anyone the opportunity to ask: "Say, who are you, anyway?" Only once did I ever hear him even come close to an explanation of his presence in the community: "Who I am is not important. What is important is that justice be served."

Yet we all knew how the show would end. The evil ones would be captured, harmony would ensue, and a crowd would gather as the mystery cowboy and Tonto rode from the scene, leaving behind that legendary symbolic silver bullet. We waited motionless for the inevitable question from some dusty cowpoke in the assembly: "By the way, who was that masked man?"

Yes, tell us! Tell us what only we know. Tell us the secret we have smugly kept the entire preceding thirty minutes of our lives.

"Why, pardner, that's the Lone Ranger!" Right! Some mental door slams securely shut. He is the man. He did the deed. He gets the credit—even though he chooses once again not to be present for the applause. We love him for that. We admire his humility. We sit in awe of how task-focused this freelance pony policeman is, disinterested in basking in the glory that his work deserves. Well, maybe he basks privately. L.R. liked knowing he did well, and just as likely he enjoyed knowing that he was getting credit for his work. Amazingly, he always showed up right at the cutting edge of his notoriety, so that most who encountered him were uninformed as to his reputation and puzzled by his black mask and white hat. It was always his final exit and his unique trademark that sparked public awareness of his full power and fame. No one knew him while he was around; everyone knew him when he was gone.

As a boy of nine, I wanted to be the Lone Ranger. Actually, I didn't want to *be* the Lone Ranger, but rather *like* him in two ways: I admired his compassion and aggressive

response to the needs of the underdog, and I was absolutely captivated by his disappearance from the scene once the job was done. I didn't fully understand all of the ramifications of heroism or mission or duty; much less did I have any clear appreciation for why L.R. chose to live that way.

But I did have several roughly carved intuitions about this masked character. Like, I saw the power of a logo. His was a silver bullet. Zorro left a "Z" carved on a tree or on someone's nicely ironed shirt. Tarzan had a yell that simultaneously stampeded elephants and stopped ivory hunters dead in their tracks. The Cross of Jesus. The Star of David, Old Glory, The Hammer and Sickle of Russia could each freeze emotions of wonder and respect in me. And no one could doubt who was present when we heard that chilling intro: "Who knows what evil lurks in the hearts of men?"

I wanted a great logo. I dreamed of a handle or nickname or symbol that would set me apart from all other inhabitants of the planet. "The one and only" dream of a boy became a recurring preoccupation of mine. I knew my name was a kind of marker that set me apart. But I also knew at least three other guys in my school who had the same first name and two others with my last name. Nothing there. My face? Nothing special. My seat in class? "And now, ladies and gentlemen, we present to you number twenty-three, fifth desk, sixth row back!" Not exactly a memory-maker.

I suspected I had to do something to be outstanding, which meant have a reputation for being really great at some sport or job or hobby or skill. I knew that my time had not yet come, for there was nothing about my life that the evening news would pick up on and splash across the airwaves.

"We interrupt this program to bring you an important news item: whatshisname went to school today and after a lunch of one bologna sandwich and a banana finished reading his assignment and went home to feed his dog before going to bed. We now return to our regularly

4

scheduled program." Nobody ever said that about the masked man or Jesus.

The second intuition taking shape in my juvenile brain was the concept of instrument. Not the word, but the concept. I was already beginning to formulate that wondrous sense of how a person can act not just for his own gain or success or fame but also for a cause or glory far greater than himself. And how while working for an ideal or good larger than his own personal interests, he can come to believe that a power greater than he is operating through him, using his skills and talents without taking anything away from the integrity of the person being used—as an instrument, as a vehicle for impacting the world around him. Like in the prayer of St. Francis: "Lord, make me an instrument of your peace."

Wow! What a reality leap! Don't get me wrong. I was no child genius. I was, at nine, not even bright enough to be labeled an underachiever. I was a bumbling asthmatic whose thinking skills were scrambled with confusion, dyslexia, and a literalness devoted to the belief that every word could have only one definition. I lived with the constant shame that the dictionary was a useless resource to me because I couldn't spell well enough to "look it up."

But there are some things you can just know—like the marketing potential of a good logo and instrumentality. I would stare mystified at Ms. Jones, my math teacher. Her chalked hand would woodpecker across the blackboard, bringing numbers to magical expressions of addition, subtraction, and mind-boggling multiplication. She would flash cards before us as the class chanted in almost perfect unison the correct math computation. I say "almost perfect unison" because there was one guy in the class who was mentally blurred by the process but whose timing was such that he could catch the tonal direction of the answer and could chime in the response only one-eighth beat behind everyone else—thus mimicking rather than knowing the solution. I can't recall ever getting caught at it.

Ms. Jones didn't just do math. She wasn't just a math whiz. To me, Ms. Jones *was* math. Her voice was nines, her legs were twos, her fingers were fives, her nose was one. She saw the world as add-ons and take-aways, and this times that. Her hair was square, her shape a triangle, her mouth a circle. She was the very personification of mathematics.

At least, that's how I saw her. I believed that in some strange way she too entered the classroom each day for the sake of math, to bring us math, to share the truths of math bequeathed to her by a former master, a higher mathgod. She was the instrument of mathness, the womanly presence of a power beyond the earth I knew. And though I rarely understood her, I respected her and what she stood for.

The bell clanged. (It didn't ring or buzz; it clanged!) Down the hall we would half walk, for the sake of rules, and half run, for the sake of whim. On to art. I was last table, back wall, with two other alphabet tailgates. There before us in apron and bunned hair stood our next goddess, Ms. Dupree. Her hands were always stained with reds and blues and grays. Her arms were dusty clay. It was she who showed us that a face was neither white nor pink nor black nor brown nor yellow but that it contained all colors. From her we learned that leaves were more than green, that a vanishing point was to be respected like a father, that a light bulb was also a mold for clown heads, that a wash was something other than clothes cleaning.

I loved her. She was art. She was a mystical butterfly that landed on our noses twice a week, tickled our fantasies, shared with us the divine secrets of color and shape, texture and size, perspective and form. She was instrumental in my awakening to a visual appreciation of the world around me.

So went my reality at nine. The police officer driving past was the law. The mayor of town was politics. The doctor we visited was the instrument of health, the dentist (in 1949) the instrument of pain. So for me, theology, or at least religion, was a piece of cake. As I sat in a hard pew at church, I listened attentively to the bible reading of Jesus saying to his disciples: "I am the Way and the Truth and the Life." Of course! I knew perfectly well what Jesus was talking about. Ms. Jones or Ms. Dupree or Officer Landry could say the same about their own instrumental lives: that a power of reality lives through them for the sake of love, order, beauty, or justice. That a woman or man can so personalize her or his own job or skill that the individual comes to stand for something grander than himself—that was no puzzlement for me. It just made sense.

It would be years before I began to doubt my perceptions and my conclusions. Had I attributed more to these talented people than was there, more than they intended, more than was humanly possible? Had my own imagination and wishing it were so carried me beyond the real powers of real people? For years I grappled with the issues of human limits, divine inspiration, prophecy, the Ouija phenomenon, career dreams, animal intelligence, paranoid delusions, destiny, free will, evolution, and the slight possibility that we humans, caught in the soup of our own creation, just might not have the last word on all that we are and what our potential is.

I'm still wondering. But as I wonder, a few things are getting clearer for me. I am learning that it is immensely rewarding and fulfilling to do something well, knowing that I have gone beyond the minimum requirements, that I have paid attention to details in such a way that not only is a task beautifully accomplished, but that I too am personally transformed from laborer to engineer, from builder to artist, from knowledge to wisdom. It is also getting clearer for me that truly great people are in fact ordinary people like Ms. Jones and Ms. Dupree and me, who enjoy enhancing in some small way the struggle of life, who take full responsibility for their efforts, and who know they are part of a larger community effort.

And finally, I am learning that it is immensely pleasurable to do well and be found out, to raise the eyebrows of those we teach, those we help, and those we love. It is great fun to have them hold that silver bullet I have left behind and hear them reminisce: "Say, pardner, who was that masked man...?"

*Afterthought*   So. Where have our heroes gone?

Better yet, where has our sense of the heroic gone?

Is there anyone out there we admire anymore?

Do we know so much about our fragile human nature that we suspect everyone's motive?

Are we becoming so cynical that we fail to notice people doing their jobs well?

What are we afraid of losing if we acknowledge someone's competence or goodness?

Does each of us know that somebody out there admires some part of us—and that we are that person's hero?

# I Didn't Want to Kill It

*Forethought*   Boys love to build things. Boys also love to take things apart, spread things around, organize things, count things, and destroy things. There lives within the masculine heart the urge not only to know what is there, but also to know we can have an impact on what is there. We want to know that things can be changed through our effort, our presence.

An extreme version of this drive to alter the world around us is the rush that comes in taking a life. Killing something that is alive is the ultimate and irreversible experience of impacting another and knowing one's power—for boys. How we deal with this primitive impulse partly determines the kind of men we become, if we ever make it to manhood.

The following account describes how one man remembers the saga of his hunting instinct and the questions it raised in his life.

W arm, friendly, comforting. These are the words that I mentally ascribe to my coffee mug as I hug it with both hands. Even more than its flavor, I think of coffee's primary contribution to my life as hot. Coffee without hot is like jalapeño without hot. The adjective is dominant to the noun. For all the awful-tasting coffee that I have drunk in my life, flavor is forgivable in the presence of hot.

Especially on this mid-December morning at one of my favorite cafes. It is unusually cold out today, and the coffee, neutral in taste, is lovingly hot to my hands and tummy. As I pause in my reading of *Alice in Wonderland* I am jolted by a comment from the booth behind me:

"Did you kill anything?"

"You bet, a doe and a seven-point racker."

"God! I'm jealous."

"Warm up on your coffee?" my waitress inquires, having appeared out of nowhere in a way that only waitresses can. I nod, unable to answer her because of a sudden lump in my throat. This past weekend one of my fellow cafe customers had huddled around a campfire with four other hunters, sipping hot coffee, planning the morning hunt—and I wasn't there. He was among the hunting men of the world; I was home raking leaves, like a young boy. He is now claiming his kill, reaping the admiration of his peers; I am in the next booth, reading *Alice in Wonderland*.

My mind goes tumbling down a seemingly bottomless hole as I recall a scene from my childhood. My father and older brother are standing in black rubber boots in our flooded backyard, while I watch from the safety of the porch steps. Marsh rats, as much as two pounds each, are swimming out from the tunnels in which they had been wintering. Dad is blasting away with his "rat gun," a .22-caliber shotgun—sometimes called our rifle—perfectly designed to fire pellet-loaded .22 shells, accurate up to thirty-five feet. He hands the rat gun to my brother, who proudly loads, aims, and sends another swimmer to rodent heaven.

Both my father and my brother loved that gun, and they were superb "ratters." I recall having killed one tomato paste can from twenty-feet away as it floated helplessly down our nearby drainage ditch. As for the rats, well, they had nothing to fear from me. For between shoots, I would secretly and methodically snare them with my Hav-A-Hart trap and release them some distance away at our town reservoir.

Growing up in southeast Texas offered us ample opportunity for duck hunting, deer hunting, dove hunting, squirrel hunting, and coon hunting. But whereas boys at school exchanged stories of weekend hunts with their dads and uncles, I withheld my own tales of an occasional rat being blasted away in our backyard. I never got invited on real hunting trips, never got to shoot with the men. So my only early familiarity with firearms occurred in scouting, when at summer camp I earned my "rifling" merit badge. That same summer I also earned my "tracking and stalking" merit badge. The two badges were sewn next to each other on my sash, and throughout my few scouting years, an unending tension existed between them.

At special meetings and full dress outings when I reluctantly donned my sash, other scouts, undoubtedly from hunter families, would touch my rifling badge and exclaim, "Good going!" Next to it, my tracking badge sat humbly silent, unrecognized and usually unidentifiable by most scouts. In fact, I never met another scout who had earned an award in tracking and stalking. For I lived surrounded by a world of shotguns, rifles, pistols, and knives by boys who loved to kill the very wildlife I loved to study. They loved the trophy, the meal, and the age-old adventure of brotherly bonding in the hunt and in the story. They praised one badge; I was more proud of the other.

For a brief moment in my early adolescence, I was fascinated with and became quite expert at the one weapon I truly admired—the bow and arrow. Three years of progressing from toy bows to powerful target bows did, in fact, stir my imagination to hunt in a more primitive manner. I speculated that I could at least give game more advantage by using a weapon that demanded exceptional skills.

But because of my skill and the electric power pole that stood near our home, I never got around to testing my humane hunting theory. My brother and I were warned repeatedly by our parents never to even think of climbing that pole because of its danger. Every other kid in the neighborhood had received the same threat from his parents. Yet during one of my target practicing sessions on a crisp fall day, my brother, for reasons as uncomplicated as "because it's there," impulsively bolted for that pole and began his ascent. I was shocked and terrified for his safety, and when he ignored my and several friends' screams to stop, I, equally impulsively, decided to stop him the only way I could. From forty yards away, I aimed for his ass and let fly a brass-tipped target arrow without the slightest doubt about my accuracy.

I was off by three inches. The arrow pierced his jacket and stuck in his belt. He stopped. I will never forget the look of shock and rage on his face as he screamed, "You shithead! You could've killed me!" Only the presence of other kids prevented him from killing me. I doubt he even heard my defense, "I didn't plan to kill you. I was just trying to stop you!"

It was in that event that I realized no animal had a fair advantage when faced by someone truly skilled with a weapon, even a bow. The ability to kill from a distance, so supremely represented in history first by the spear, then the bow, and now the rifle, cannon, and missile, carries a supreme responsibility of protecting others—beasts and human alike—from our destructive potential. The further removed we have come from face-to-face assault and hand-to-hand struggle, the more removed we are from claiming responsibility for our actions. "The gun went off." "I wasn't aiming at her." "Someone pushed a button to fire it." The human mental trick of denying direct and immediate connection with an instrument that comes to have a mind of its own and thus a will of its own is the ultimate posture of lethal irresponsibility. Like other thirteen year olds, I was fascinated by the lure of weapons and the mystery of power they represented. But as I stood there holding my bow and feeling intimately connected to it that fateful autumn day, I was also terrified by both my skill and my power: I could have killed my brother to save him from death.

On a similar fall morning some twenty years later, my nine-year-old son and I walked stealthily through the piney woods of east Texas. The previous afternoon he had been more impressed with my instructions on firing a .22-caliber rifle than he was with my uncommon knowledge of tracking and stalking squirrel. Today he carried the weapon excitedly as I whispered my observations of lush beech groves, shredded pine cones, nesting, and an occasional squirrel's chatter. And although he respectfully nodded his head as I spoke, I could see that his attention was riveted on the trigger he was fingering and the anticipated live target he would soon see.

It was he who spotted the squirrel scurrying across the top branches of a majestic water oak. He walked directly under the animal in order to get a shot and, without a word exchanged between us, went through his newly learned sequence of aim, safety off, breath, aim, fire. The squirrel dropped to the ground two feet in front of my son. He stood there, staring at the now dead animal, and, with tears in his eyes, said, "I didn't want to kill it; I just wanted to see if I could hit it." I held him as he cried.

It was a magical moment for both a father and a son. Before he had pulled the trigger, his driving question had been: Can I hit it? After he pulled the trigger, his nagging wonder was: Did I intend this outcome, this squirrel's death? He had stepped not from boyhood to manhood but from fantasy to reality. He had touched his own power to kill at a distance; he had experienced the remorse of unintentionally taking a life. And I wondered if he could possibly hold on to these realities in the midst of peer congratulations and the competitive spirit that awaited us at the cabin.

Like a scene painted on some ancient cave wall, a celebration dance was underway. Young hunters, clad in leather and plaid, held their squirrel trophies high as they paraded proudly into the sacred fire area. Mothers and sisters rushed to applaud the young men while fathers stood apart, beaming a pride that needed no words. We instructed

14

the boys in the arts of knife use, skinning, and preparing the small animals for cooking. We laughed as the stories swelled in size and drama.

At dinner that cold December night, fried squirrel was heaped in a large pan at the table's center. All the young hunters eagerly reached for their captured meat. But while others ate heartily, I sipped my hot coffee and watched as my son ate around his squirrel leg, and I imagined him thinking, "I knew who I was when I woke up this morning, but I must have changed several times since then."

"More coffee, sir?" my waitress asks. I nod and mouth a silent "thank you" so as to not disrupt my eavesdropping on the grown boys in the next booth. For one, it was his eleventh buck; for another, his twenty-third kill.

I was lost again, this time in my past weekend trip from Austin with my wife. We had developed a tradition of finding a local barbecue hovel and treating ourselves to a sandwich of juicy fare. And on this route we were chosen by "Billy Bob's Bar-B-Q" in Hempstead, Texas. As we entered the cafe, we were stunned by the numerous mounted trophies that filled the walls: deer, elk, bobcat, cougar, bear, and even a buffalo.

"Where's Billy Bob?" I asked as we moved our trays along the cafeteria-style rails.

"You're looking at him," beamed a tall and well-stuffed halfback of fifty-something.

"Mr. Bob," I said, "I've got a question for you, if you don't mind."

"Shoot," he invited back.

I pointed to the four heavily populated walls and half-joked, "Just how many is enough?"

Billy laughed. "Hell, man, it ain't never enough. Every kill is like the first time."

"You got that right!" I deceitfully agreed. Then I pushed a bit: "But, did you ever spend the day tracking a herd of deer, stalking them without being detected, and be so close you could hear their breathing and see into their eyes, and decide to photograph rather than kill one?"

Billy Bob's jaw ground left, then right, then left again. And with a look that had for forty years squelched all emotion inside him, stated, "You want beans or potato salad?"

He could not know that I harbored no resentment nor disdain nor criticism of sport hunters. Billy Bob could not possibly appreciate how much we held in common: our love for the wilderness, our knowledge of wildlife, our fascination with humankind's relationship with all other life forms, our sense of power, and our fascination with our own ability to kill at a distance. He could only surmise that I was a member of Save-the-Whatever organization come to hassle and embarrass him in the privacy of his own hall of trophies, foolishly mistaking a portrait shot for a mounted rack.

Billy Bob's barbecue was tasty and hot; "Billy Bob's Bar-B-Q" was as cold as death. As we rose to leave our table and walked toward the door, I noticed for the first time above the entrance a deer rifle lying in the up-turned forelegs and hooves of a doe. And above the rifle was mounted a large trophy photograph of Mr. Camouflage himself, Billy Bob. I grinned as I elbowed my wife, who whispered back, "Score one for the deer!"

"More coffee?" intrudes my waitress, as my daydreams fade.

"No thanks," I reply. "I've heard enough."

*Afterthought*   So. Do we men hunt for the same reasons we hunted as boys?

Does hunting teach us something about becoming a man? If so, what?

How do we balance hunting with our respect for life?

To what degree have we disowned personal responsibility when we use a weapon that can harm at a distance?

Can we find ways to impact our world without doing violence to it?

Are there ways, other than killing, we guys can be together and compete in adult rituals?

Does the ultimate feminine experience of creating life offer a balance to us men and our impulse to kill?

# Just Tell Me How

*Forethought*     Long before the information explosion of the late twentieth century, humankind has known that knowledge is power. We have struggled with just what to do with knowledge, how it is gained, owned, traded, shared, and used to control others. Boys grow up craving knowledge about how to make things work, how the universe is glued together, how to dazzle and taunt one another with, "I know something you don't know."

    The author of the following essay has obviously thought long and hard on how his fellow men have guarded their acquired treasures of information, how they barter for prestige with their data, and how they tease one another with their secrets. He hints at the bond of love that is found among men who share their wisdom, and the frustration and alienation that surround men who must learn alone.

We had been blessed with a clear spring day as our van arrived at Gilmore Bay in northern Minnesota. Sightings of deer, eagles, beaver huts, and even a gray wolf had highlighted our day's travel to the lake. Earlier in the day we had visited an area fishing tackle store, a habit I had developed through years of fishing in new places. Who else

talks to local fishermen and women as much as the town tackle shop manager?

So McDougle's Sport Center, a forty- by forty-five-foot brick structure next to the local liquor store, was my intended source of fishing information. Following the usual polite "hellos," I got right to the point:

"We're from out of state and have never fished here. Could you tell us how to fish the lake area and what I might buy here to make it all happen?"

A blank face was struggling to respond. Our lone teenage attendant apologized that the owner was out having coffee and would return within an hour; but he, being an occasional lure-tosser, would offer some "guesses" as to what might work in the lakes. We didn't have an hour; he didn't have the information. Disheartened, I purchased thirty-five dollars worth of guesses, and we were on our way.

Standing near the boat launch at Gilmore Bay, my spirits were up. The smell of reed-soaked water, red-winged blackbirds shattering through cattail groves, white pelicans soaring in formation overhead—all contributed to my excitement about the coming days of enjoying lodge living and family fun. The lodge owner and his son signaled us to approach and began loading our luggage onto their nineteen-foot Chriscraft boat for the eight-mile jaunt to the lodge. This man, I surmised to myself, will undoubtedly be able and eager to answer my angling questions. It's his job to create a wonderful experience for his guests. He knows the lake. He fishes here.

Upon arrival at the lodge and settling in, I respectfully inquired as to when we might have a conference on the lake. Whisking out the screen door, our resident leader replied in respectful but more solemn tones:

"Not an easy lake; but we'll talk about her later."

Next to the door was a sign: "Guide $175. Inquire within." My heart sank for the second time. One hundred seventy-five dollars! Suddenly a new political twist surrounded me: Do I have to pay extra for the information I desire, or is the data included in the price of the lodging? Do I get amateur info free and professional info at a dear price? And because we are just vacation guests, are we automatically grouped among the unenlightened and perhaps undeserving? Should we have registered as trophy hunters rather than city escapees?

Like lost children waiting for our room assignment in our temporary foster home, my family and I walked about the premises, hands in pockets, eyes assessing our surroundings. I began to reflect on the rather odd situation in which I found myself. Having flown halfway across the country to spend six days at a fishing lodge nestled on the shore of an unfamiliar lake the size of New Jersey, preparing to chase down species of fish I had never even seen before in my life, wanting to spend at least half our time exploring the fauna and flora of the area, and being the dubious owner of thirty-five dollars' worth of tackle guesses, I became acutely aware that I had neither the time nor the energy to approach fishing this tree- and rock-studded ocean on a trial-and-error basis.

I needed information. Not definitely exact information, but current and relevant information. I needed lake structure information, weather information, license information, boat information. How do we fish for northern pike, what does a walleye prefer for lunch, what time do smallmouth bass forage for breakfast in these cold waters, where do the muskie hide, when do we spare the rods, and when can I best expect to spoil the fishing child in me?

Given sufficient time, opportunity, and favorable conditions, we could have eventually answered on our own all of these questions. But these three precious commodities of time, opportunity, and favorable conditions are the very items we didn't have during our too brief stay on Moose Lake. I thought of an ancient Chinese proverb: "Feed a man a fish, he eats once; teach him to fish, he eats a lifetime."

I don't remember when I first learned to fish, but I suspect it was around the age of eight, under the supervision of my uncle Carlo, for it was with him I frequently fished, hunted frogs, and changed the inner tubes of my bike. I asked in order to learn; he gave, out of his desire to teach and share. Thirty-five years later it was he who by long distance telephone also walked me through the process of flaring the copper tubing I was replacing on our water heater. He had the information I needed and he took the time to share it with me. All I had to do was create the opportunity to learn. We never thought of cost. He never forgot to add: "Have fun. That's what we're here for."

Now there is cost, usually in the form of money. Everywhere I turn in my life somebody owns information I want, is prepared to sell it to me at a particular price, and demands that I comply with conditions favorable to him or her before I can have the information. Is $175 per day a fair price for limited but "professional" fishing information? Is $175 per hour a fair price for legal information? Is $175 per minute a fair price for surgery? I don't know anymore; the decimal point eludes me.

Computer technology has certainly helped focus our attention on the cost and the relative value of information. But long before this electronic wizardry came along, I was aware that information could be translated into power, skill, and dollars. I've always admired craftspeople, from carpenters to artists to architects to nurses to teachers. Every profession, every trade, even every hobby has its own body of knowledge. And I've always been enchanted with how each practitioner guards that information as if the information had a life and a price tag of its own. The trading of information through services and products carries the illusion that the information is *in* the product. It is not. Real information, live information, relevant information is in people.

To some degree objects do carry some data inside. A thousand years from now, a Minnesota archeologist will unearth in this general vicinity one of my fishing lures I will likely lose this week—my River Runt. Her catalog of twentieth-century objets d'art will inform her that this product is a treasure trove of information. The plastic three-inch creature looks like a cross between a pale dung beetle and a Zulu war mask, sporting a silver nose ring and two mated treble hooks. She will surmise it was pulled through water by an attached line, while northern species of fish "read" the object's information as "bite-sized fish."

What the scientist will never discover is the information lost forever in the human experience of this Runt. She will never retrieve the fact that while the lure was invented for and sold primarily around northern lakes for northern fish, this product also was widely distributed in the southern United States. And when pulled with a line through southern waters before the discriminating noses of southern fish, the lure was consistently and accurately identified as a plastic Zulu dung beetle. There is no record of it ever being misread as "food" by a Texas bass, crappie, or catfish.

Purchased in 1951, this particular R.R. sailed through the air and slammed into water 3,647 times, caught twenty-seven tons of weeds and sticks, and punctured my body no fewer than thirty times. And what lure manufacturer would pay me $175 for that kind of live information? Amazingly, I still had the Runt, tired and cast-worn, tucked in my tackle box as a good-luck charm.

We strolled out to the boat dock and introduced ourselves to Don, the boat keeper. He greeted us warmly and advised us that a fully equipped johnboat and motor would be ready when we were, and that he would supply us with all the worms we needed. Now I was getting somewhere. At least I was able to apply the cardinal rule of fishing: When all else fails, try worms. He also assured us that once we had acquired a lake map in the lodge store for $1.75, he would point out where fish were being caught in the area.

This man I could love. He appreciates that a map is a cornucopia of information at a very low cost. I treasure maps, for a good map tells me where I am in relation to my surroundings, what direction I must travel, how far my destination is, what choice of routes are available to me. With this information, I can better portion out that most precious commodity, time, and I can more freely negotiate travel conditions as well as points of interest. Finally, with a good map I may still get lost, but I won't stay lost.

It was not, however, a good map. It was, as my wife called it, a fill-it-in-as-you-go-along map, so by the end of our stay our map would have been the envy of any visitor to the lake. It was transformed into a $17.50 map. We inquired at other lodges, we interviewed licensing officials, customs officials, fishermen and their wives. We recorded depth readings, wind directions, wildlife habitat data, shoreline configurations, feeding times and conditions, fish locations. We had as much fun with our map building as we did with any other event that week.

Perhaps I was being too critical of our lodge owner and his staff. Maybe fishermen really are not that stingy with information. It just may be in the nature of humankind that we guard carefully the information we have, share it sparingly, and never give a full disclosure without expecting some compensation or extracting some trade for our hard-earned data. On occasion, we may delight in making a task a bit easier for someone and may be willing to offer some free tips.

But unconsciously we fear two things: having our information stolen from us without adequate recognition or compensation for our work, and giving someone else a competitive edge with our information. We want credit for the maps each of us has drawn in life, and we don't want our maps being used against us. So we create standards, certifications, licenses, degrees, positions, ranks, classes, castes, and uniforms to identify all manner of information ownership. We look to shoulder patches, hats, wall hangings, and price tags to tell us who has the data we need for a particular service or product, and what it will cost us. And we share a socially accepted delusion that the higher the price, the better the information.

Perhaps things have not always been so severely competitive. Perhaps before the Industrial Revolution of western civilization, when the pace of life was slower, when agrarian skills dominated, when communities were smaller, and when a more personal exchange among family, friends, and neighbors allowed us to know one another, information was more easily shared. Then interdependence was more highly valued than independence, giving more cherished than receiving, sharing more common than owning, learning more honored than possessing.

Perhaps our growing separation through specialization, rising costs, and family dismemberment forces us to collect more and more dollars to purchase more and more information we need in order to isolate ourselves even more from having to depend on one another. Cost has become the price of civilization.

Because we have evolved to the point of generating and needing so much information, and because we don't have those precious commodities of time, opportunity, and adequate conditions to learn on our own what we need in order to fish the overwhelming number of lakes in which we live, information specialization is what we do. It's all we can do in a brief lifetime—to learn well only one or two fishing skills for a limited number of lakes.

So each man guards well what he does well, and he sells his information at the best market price. He competes daily against men with similar skills, and he strives to make himself the best in his field. His share of the market represents his success, his prowess, and his survival. Ultimately, his success is also a prime marketing device for mate attraction and support of offspring. What a world! It's a world populated by men, each of whom carries wherever he goes a small box containing a collection of photographs of his finest catches and the remnants of his most successful lures, eagerly awaiting to say seductively to the next woman, "Want to see some interesting pictures?"

And women? Do they gather, hoard, and sell information? Sarah's Lodge was within walking distance of our camp. We strolled over to buy our visiting fishing licenses and to chat about the area. As she was filling out legal forms, I posed my standard question:

"Say, Sarah, how do we fish this lake?"

Sarah stopped in the midst of her marginal profit task and replied:

"Easy. Worms and leeches on the bottom, off rock points for walleye. That red and white skirt spoon you already have is fine for pike: Troll near shallow grass beds. Don't waste your time on muskie or your money on a guide. Too iffy. Best morning lure around for smallmouth is a River Runt. Sells for $1.75, but here, use mine. And don't worry if you lose 'im. Have fun. That's what you're here for."

*Afterthought*  So. Who are the teachers in our lives, those who took the time to share with us and loved doing it?

Have we thanked our mentors, our guides for all they have given us?

Have we ever noticed the tension that we feel between our excitement to share immediately a discovery and our fear of loss of status or prestige once we give that knowledge away to the world?

What information have we withheld from people we love, information that could help them deal with us more effectively, more lovingly?

How can we know what information should be kept secret, what should be sold or bartered, what should be given away?

How do we know when someone is ready to receive what we know?

# *Choose Me, Choose Me Not*

*Forethought*  Ever had trouble deciding which car to buy, which road to take, whether this was the right job? Of course—we all have. Ever wondered if other people had less difficulty making decisions, whether they always knew what they wanted, whether they were more satisfied with their lots in life? Certainly we all know that everyone else is saner, clearer, happier.

My grandma once said that we live with two recurring fears in our lives: one, that we won't be noticed; the other, that we will be noticed. Having mixed feelings *is* the human condition. Feeling torn between equally powerful impulses and ideas is our struggle, even though this struggle does not fit our preferred image of ourselves. Rarely do we have the clarity and conviction of: "Give me liberty, or give me death!" Usually it's: "Give me liberty, or…uh…OK, don't give me liberty. Whatever!"

Our next writer speaks beautifully to this indecision that shadows us through life. Maybe you'll enjoy his story. Maybe not.

It was the dream again. Halfway through brushing my teeth it came to me. Tulane University, student-faculty lounge, senior year, choosing finalists to represent the school. The opportunity of a lifetime to travel, make career connections, to compete in one of the most prestigious contests in higher education: the National Collegiate Debate.

For three-and-a-half years I had prepared for and dreamed of this moment. My studies in biology seemed almost a sideline to my interest in logic, communication skills, and the debate club. I had been encouraged by faculty and students alike who saw in me skills I never knew I possessed. At times I could not separate in my mind their urgings from my own interest. I was carried along by both. Winning or losing a debate held little interest for me when compared with the very process of mental exchange, challenge, and pursuit.

The dream takes many forms. But always it remains unfinished, with an unanswered question: "Would I have been chosen?" For the real life event that gives life to the dream was my untimely leaving of school before the final selection took place. A death had occurred, calling me away from the university, disrupting my studies, and delaying even my graduation for another year. The magical moment was lost in events I could not control. Twenty-five years later I am, on occasion, still having the dream, still asking the question: "Would I have been chosen?"

The debate-team-opportunity-lost is not the only event that stirs the dream. But without doubt, it represents and summarizes somewhere in the deeper recesses of my heart a larger collection of powerful moments in my life when I stood wondering and wavering in the face of choosing or being chosen. How clever of my mind, which has a mind of its own, to have chosen the metaphor of debate to represent to itself and to me this array of life experiences surrounding my lifelong struggle with ambivalence.

In another version of the dream I am seated at my desk in a classroom of other nine or ten year olds. My arm is stretched high in the air, my hand waving, my other arm supporting the first. Many hands are up, so it is safe for mine

to be up. Many hands are waving, so I can inconspicuously wave mine. Many faces smile and eyes shine in their eagerness to answer the teacher's question, so I blend in with an animated face of, "Pick me, pick me!"

She had just asked: "Class, what is the soul?"

I know, I know. Pick me. Her eyes scan the little forest of arms. Mrs. Dillard loved to take her time, allowing the excitement to grow, trying to be fair, often ferreting out the hidden face of a distracted classmate, a sleeper, a cutup, a triple "S" (strategically studious stare).

"Sally…"

Moan. Not her again. Of course ol' Dillard would pick the class brain. Of course she would skip me on the one question I could finally answer. Naturally, my one chance to shine would be robbed from me, forever, by the likes of Sally Anne. Rally Sally stands.

"The soul is the spiritual part of us that never dies and joins God in heaven."

"Excellent, Sally. When we are born, our soul…"

I lose track of what the teacher is saying because I'm in shock. I can hardly breathe, yet I feel strangely relieved, like I have just been rescued from being burned at the stake. I can't believe my good luck because I was going to answer:

"The sole is the bottom part of the shoe."

Had our teacher chosen me, I would have been the laughing stock of the class. I would have worn the dunce's cap the entire year, been the butt of sole jokes, been encouraged by the fiendish souls in my class to volunteer even more idiotic responses to questions I had not a clue how to answer.

No, I had barely escaped the death of ridicule even in the midst of my absolute certainty as to the correct answer. Dare I ever again hold up my hand and risk being chosen if I have any doubt about what is being asked of me? This near-death experience carried a warning: certainty can be achieved only after the fact, at which time it is safe to announce, "I knew that!"

Unfortunately, being the slow learner that I was, my childhood and adolescence were punctuated by my volunteering for jobs I had not the slightest idea how to perform, of agreeing to run for offices I could not manage, and allowing divinely inspired adults to use me in capacities totally foreign to my skills and interests.

Did I just look so unbelievably gullible? Was I craving to be included at any cost? Was there a streak of the daredevil in me that kept revealing itself in spite of my self-image of a cautious and blundering post-factum sage? Certainly I failed at as many endeavors as I succeeded, probably more. So surely I was not born to be chosen, born to lead, or born to excel. It was more that I was obsessed with having to say some version of "yes" to invitations to step forward while at the same time holding onto a terror of being found out as inept in the task.

What puzzled me was the haunting realization that throughout my willingness to let myself be selected for this and that, I never was clear about whether or not I wanted to do any of the tasks. Did I want to earn that badge in scouting or was I fulfilling the requirements because the scoutmaster said it was time? Did I enter the fire prevention contest because I chose to or was it the only activity offered me in class? Was I selected to attend the Junior Red Cross summer camp because of my excitement for emergency operations or because I was the ranking male in the club? Was I elected president of my senior class because of my leadership skills and my wish to enhance student body involvement in school decisions, or was it because no one else wanted the job and I got nudged forward by default—maybe even as a class joke?

By the time I was entering college, I had developed an array of responses to invitations—responses that roughly substituted for "yes, I want to" without actually saying, "yes, I want to"—while at the same time negating the possibility of my ever knowing if I wanted to. These responses included: "If you want to," "Why not?" "OK," "That would be nice,"

"Whatever you say," and "I'll be there." The last was my favorite, for it usually proved true that by showing up, I would get the job. Whether or not I wanted the job never surfaced as an issue.

Imagine going through life without ever using the two most important words in language: "Yes" and "No." Imagine never revealing to yourself or to anyone else what you genuinely thought or felt about an issue or event, never saying what you wanted: "That's interesting. That will work. It's up to the group. What can I say? Don't ask me! Whatever is called for. Somebody's gotta do it. Let's get started. I'll take it on. I'll try. I think I can. Give me a shot at it. Why me? Why not me?"

Never "yes," never "no." Nothing changed in adulthood. I was asked, "Do you take this woman to be your lawfully wedded wife?" Thank God I was never asked if I *wanted* to marry her: I could not have answered. What seemed clear and certain was that she had chosen me. Wasn't that sufficient for the deal? Besides, I now had post-factum certainty that she must, in fact, love me, want me, insist on including me. I could completely delete what I wanted. I accepted the arrangement. It seemed timely, appropriate, socially approved.

In the hospital waiting room, I was told: "Sir, your wife has given birth to a healthy daughter." I was not asked if I wanted to be the father of a daughter. A man does not exactly decide to become a father. He decides to engage in sexual activity with the woman who chose to marry him. She chooses motherhood. The child chooses the dad. The dad chooses to look and sound appropriately happy, while choking back a wave of fear and weightiness that engulfs his sense of dutiful posture. Did I now, after the fact, want to be a father? Of course. Notice my arm held high, my hand waving, my animated face. The masked nurse, looking a lot like Mrs. Dillard, nods approvingly through the nursery window.

A third recurring dream comes to mind. I'm standing in an ice cream parlor that serves forty-one flavors, and I am as frozen in my indecision as the ice cream is in its waiting. An attendant approaches.

"What can I get you?" he asks politely.

"What's good? " I respond, hardly believing the idiocy of my own words. He laughs; everyone in the place laughs. I pretend a laugh. Hoping to narrow the problem to a manageable size I inquire:

"What's the flavor of the month? " The attendant spots my stall and responds:

"What do you want? "

Now he has me. Trapped. What do I want? Well, I want not to inconvenience the man. I want not to hold up the growing line of customers behind me. I want not to look and sound like a fool. I want to appear decisive, clear, even in charge. What stumps me is what flavor I want. Do I try something new? Fall back on what I forced myself into selecting the time before, if I could just remember the time before? Further delay the process by asking for a taste or three? Capitulate to old reliable vanilla?

There is no end in sight to my confusion and immobility. What if I choose the wrong one—as if somehow there might be a wrong one? What if I don't like my choice? Perhaps I should surround the chance of error by selecting three or four kinds, thereby minimizing my potential disappointment. Nuts may stick in my teeth. Some flavors are overpowering, fruit imitations bland, blended flavors cancel each other out, single flavors unexciting. And what about fat content, cholesterol count, stabilizers and preservatives, the seduction of toppings and sprinkles?

Through this whirling dervish of considerations I glimpse the attendant's fingers tapping out a pre-execution drum roll; I hear feet shuffling behind me, deep sighs, someone asking, "Anybody bring a newspaper?"

"Strawberry...and Homemade Vanilla!" I shout authoritatively. "Thank God," a voice whispers several heads back. Strawberry, because my dad always liked strawberry; vanilla, because I'm a coward. Had I chosen what I wanted? Everyone thought so. Only I knew the truth: the two had chosen me. For they were the two frozen canisters staring up at me where and when I was fatefully challenged to make a decision. An accident of geography, not of preference. Chance, not choice. Pressure, not passion. What, not want.

Such nightmares dreamed and daymares lived are the consequences of never learning to trust my own perceptions. I was the kid who wore a coat when my mother was cold. I pretended to love cabbage when Aunt Nell visited. I accepted the blousy shirts my grandma made me. I said I liked school. I looked brave "going first." When at six I was given an opportunity to taste my grandfather's muscatel wine, my mother frowned with worry, warning: "Doesn't it taste terrible? Wouldn't want you to like it and be an alcoholic like your father!" I loved the taste. I loved its warmth as it slid down my throat. I loved its sweet and bitter odor that blanketed my nose inside the glass.

My secret conclusion? I must be a confirmed alcoholic at six, like my father. And I knew that for all time I was potentially damned by the judgment of God's earthly representative, my mother. Hoping against hope, I doubled my sinfulness; I lied, desperately hurling myself at her protective approval and cruelly crushing the truth of my palate and my nose.

"Yuck. It's awful!" I announced deceitfully.

I would spend the next twenty years of my life avoiding wine and trying to convince myself that I would be an improved version of my father—for her. In a thousand ways I would choose *inclusion* over claiming the truth of what I saw, heard, felt, tasted. In every ice cream parlor for the rest of my life I would scan the list of flavors, and when asked what I wanted, I would stifle my impulse to shout: "Muscatel!"

Other people would always know better than I what I wanted, what I needed, what I preferred. So I developed a double life of sensing and judging. One of me would secretly know what I liked, while my other me would act in accord with whatever had been decided for me. One of me would recall my year in St. Mary's Orphanage as the finest year of my childhood, while my other me, in the presence of my guilt-ridden family, would recount the horrors of abandonment and abuse. One of me would listen with creative pleasure to the obscure sexual stories of my friends in school; my other me—him—would express remorse and self-hatred the following Saturday afternoon as he knelt repentantly in the church confessional.

I lived a hidden and forbidden life of seeing, feeling, and knowing the truth of my utterly human self; he lived a socially acceptable life of deceit, lies, avoidance, equivocation, and fraudulent compliance. For being accurate, clear, and truthful to my poor human self, I knew I was bad; for being cleverly adaptive and deceitfully dutiful, he was called good. Self-honesty was sinful; self-deceit was saintly. Never once in my entire childhood did I confess committing a public act of badness; my entire list of self-loathing and punishable crimes were my thoughts, my feelings, my fantasies, and my conclusions about my hidden and regrettably human self —the I that I kept separate from him, and hidden from them. I was bad for liking muscatel; he was good for lying about it.

Such a split between a good self (usually public) and a bad self (often hidden) is the springboard for so many of us men becoming early divided in our perceptions, judgments, and behavior. We learned to live two lives: the good boy who does what it takes to please his mommy and daddy, and the bad boy who takes on the neighborhood and school with his impulsive emotions and friendship-building antics. By becoming so divided, we drift further and further away from the original integrity of our birth—that position of an undivided soul, unworried about image and daring to say what we were.

We learn early in childhood that there is pain, confusion, and fear surrounding this divided self. To compensate for this pain, we learn also the great camouflage maneuver of all time: competition. What a wonderful distraction and cover-up. We construct an elaborate system of being *right* (translate: fear of being odd-guy-out), of *winning* (translate: fear of being the forgotten loser), of *succeeding* (translate: fear of loss of status and earning ridicule), and of being the *best* (translate: loss of judgment about what is adequate or good enough).

Not Good Enough. That's the darn virus that keeps showing up and contaminating our focus and our efforts. The fear of being not good enough becomes the driving force in a lifelong obsession with comparing ourselves with everyone else, impelling us to search where the light is brightest—in competition, in counting, in accumulation of money, property, people, and power—while steering us away from where the shadows lie, the hidden questions of our inner self, the division we feel inside, the unrest that robs us of personal peace and family joy.

We commit our lives to a frenzied pace of busy and hurry and volume. We would rather catch our limit of fish five times over in the fastest possible time than enjoy the pleasure of a sunrise on the river and the joyful release of a single rainbow trout.

No surprise that we reach the age of reason at about fifty, and, when asked what we want, we impulsively respond: "I guess just to continue more of what I'm doing so I can take it easy later and do more of what I want, although I'm not sure what that is."

"What do I want?" is not an easy question to answer. Preferred answers include:

    a. More of what I already have.

    b. Whatever I don't already have.

    c. Whatever he's having.

    d. The best that money can buy.

    e. My way.

Again, no surprises here. Utter silliness. Mindless dodges. But useful, nonetheless, in adding to our skills of avoiding ever knowing the secret longings of our hearts, the dreams we might have had, and the connections we could have achieved with our own lives had we stopped long enough to search those shadows.

Did I want to play football in school with my classmates? Not really. What I wanted was to be chosen on a team, to be important enough to be selected—not to have my body bashed by guys sixty pounds heavier and a foot taller than I was. Did I want loud parties, all-day beach outings in a blazing sun, class picnics of six hundred strong, being president of my church youth group, the trip to Florida, the dance with the U.S. Army, the Congressional Hearings in D.C., or the thousands of time-consuming group events in my life? No. What I wanted was *not to be left out*. More accurately, what I wanted was to be invited—not necessarily to attend.

Was I ever—really—good enough to have been chosen? Was his/her/their choice of me based on merits accurately attributed to me, or have I so successfully scammed my way through life that I managed to show up at the right time with the appropriate smile and my hand held high? Have I in fact yet claimed my own integrity, my undivided self, my authentic competence? Or have I just achieved the supreme skill of never really being found out!? And, do I know the difference?

Aging has its humorous side. How cleverly have I now traded places with the ominous "them" who I once hoped would choose me, so that now I am the "them" by whom my young colleagues want to be chosen. Oh, the slight of hand to move from the position of hopefully chosen to preferred chooser. Do I now want to choose them who want to be chosen by me? How can I, master of deceit that I have become, trust that these mere mortals speak the truth, have any real skills, can perform competently, or genuinely want the job? The whole damn thing has just worn me out!

No, we never really finish with major human issues like belonging, feeling excluded, choice, preference, and that mother of all experiences, ambivalence. I will dream again of that debate team, that high school four-year plan, that little league team I never tried out for, those other women. I will dream of the day when I no longer have to be chosen, when all choices are equally valid. I will dream of when being good enough dissolves in a heart that finally trusts that the man I am is good, not comparatively with bad, but existentially—because I am who I am, I am only what I can be. I will dream that there does not have to be a heaven, but that if there happens to be one, then entrance into heaven will be automatic. For if Peter, standing at the gate, asks me if I want to enter, I know with all the certainty of my being that those next few moments will, for me, be hell.

*Afterthought*   So. How do we live a life divided between our craving for certainty and our frustration with uncertainty?

Are we still fussing at ourselves for past decisions, past blunders, and past opportunities lost? Why?

Are we still demanding of ourselves that we have the truth, that we get it right, that we not want what we cannot have?

Has our divided self felt the urge finally to mend, to come together in that awesome experience of being truthful to one's self, before dying?

What inner struggle was Groucho Marx revealing in his famous words: "I would never join a club that would choose me as a member?"

# *Pigeons*

*Forethought*   Cops and robbers, cowboys and Indians, earthlings and aliens, Allies and Nazis, Yanks and Rebs, England and Colonists. We are at innocent moments in our lives, absolutely clear about who are the good guys and who are the bad guys. We feel righteous, even called upon to identify, attack and rid the universe of the enemy. We know that we are among the elected good and they are the unfortunate evil.

So thought our next writer, convinced as he was that his actions were for the common good. Until one day, when the weather changed, and he had time to think about his definition of the world...

It rained today. The very day I had time to be at home, to read, to work in the yard, to maybe go fishing—it rained. This unannounced, long-awaited, and much-needed shower also was hindering my current ecology project: the reduction, if not annihilation, of a growing and bothersome pigeon population in our neighborhood.

The rain reminded me that I should have cleaned the gutters. Fallen oak leaves, remnants of the daily roof slides, lay gutter-crunched and packed. Left undisturbed, they would become a prestige apartment unit for wintering slugs, spiders, various larvae and cocoons. And on a rainy fall day, this leaf impaction forces water to cascade along the entire length of this obsolete invention, rendering the gutter system useless.

For years we had cultivated flowers, trimmed hedges, mowed, set out hummingbird feeders and seed feeders alike, welcomed nesting mockingbirds and purple martins and cardinals and chickadees and yes, even sparrows. We've encouraged our squirrel neighbors, going so far as to tolerate their occasional killing of potted plants by burying a nut therein and marking it with urine. Such has been our contribution to sharing our environment with the descendants of local wildlife settlers.

But, pigeons! A good idea gone bad. No one knows the hundreds if not thousands of human enthusiasts who took nature's gem—rock dove—and, after having their fling at hobby or food production, disbanded their pens and freed into the skies one of the messiest and most ravenous members of the bird family. In roaming flocks of from thirty to three hundred strong they scour the city for food and housing, driving out other bird populations, not by hostile intent, but by the sheer and overwhelming presence of their numbers. They are immune to traps, fearless of people, and unfazed by scarecrows, scareowls, scarehawks, or any other stuffed or plastic image of their natural predators. Their very boldness has limited me to one method of limiting them: my newly acquired pellet rifle.

With the exception of my fish-and-release, fish-and-eat rule, I prefer not to kill wildlife. Yet I intimately understand the moral dilemma of an overpowering species disrupting the delicate balance of an ecosystem. The pigeon, another human endeavor gone sour, is one of those species. So one by one I send them to bird heaven, not out of pleasure, but solely to make small amends for a human error and to allow for the presence of other species in the neighborhood.

I am now four months into my pigeon endeavor. I suppose I could assuage my ill feelings about killing pigeons by telling myself that I am merely harvesting a disproportionately advantaged unit of a fragile ecosystem.

Sounds great to me. But I have spent too many cynical years on this planet to be seduced by verbally disguising a nasty human act—my own included. I kill pigeons because they are messy, arrogant, stubborn, defiant, pushy, greedy and shameless; even though I privately know that none of these accusations fairly describes a bird that is genetically programmed to simply show up for breakfast, snacks, lunch, snacks, dinner and snacks.

The task seems endless. They don't appear to be weakening in their numbers. In fact, there are more pigeons lining the power lines now than before I began my eradication project. "Wack!" goes my rifle. A gray and white victim falls deftly into my neighbor's rose bushes. Twenty-nine survivors take to the air, speeding to the safety of power lines out of rifle range. And with these sounds and sights, another hundred pigeons are alerted to a nearby meal, while their reproductive hormones begin to surge through their feathered loins. Like Adam, exercising dominion over his garden, I simultaneously trigger the death of one and excite the mating of twenty. The word has gone out among them that another human is protecting his turf, proof that he is hoarding good things to eat and is exercising an aviary prejudice against pigeons. What a challenge! What a cause! What a fool!

Our local parks and wildlife officials estimate that there is a current population of some two and a half million pigeons in the greater Houston area, with a steady growth rate of two percent per annum. My weekly kill of four pigeons is not destined to make a huge dent in a weekly birth rate of almost one thousand, so I am sure my murderous endeavor will not result in a too limited gene pool for these airborne vacuum cleaners. In fourteen thousand years of shooting their number will increase by sixty-eight trillion birds.

So, as a group, the pigeons are doing well. They love the drama. They vote for who gets to lead the next attack on the bird feeders. They observe with sneers on their beaks the futile attempts of our cats even to get within pouncing range.

They fly up and away at the now familiar sound of my pellet rifle being pumped from inside our kitchen.

*I* am not doing so well. I don't like seeing myself as a pigeon killer, I don't like owning a pellet rifle, and I live with the shame of my neighbors leering at me from their windows: "There he is, our local bird killer. Takes all kinds." And I slink about for fear that our roving security guard in one of his silent drive-bys will set off his siren, arrest me, and refuse to believe that I was only bird hunting in a metropolitan neighborhood for the good of ecology while entertaining my victims. It just doesn't look good at all. My worst nightmare is that I am dead wrong about the whole affair. Maybe the pigeons, bullybirds that they be, are not the problem. Maybe I'm just not seeing the whole picture clearly. Perhaps bird feeders should be more accurately named pigeon troughs. Those constructions covering our houses are not roofs, but pigeon potties. Power lines are pigeon roosts, and native birds are actually sub-dominant infestations—insects of the bird world.

Maybe pigeons are destined to rule the airways, as cockroaches rule the ground. And I, in my misguided efforts to stem the tide of this species, am actually accelerating their determination to overcome the forces of human tyranny and nearsightedness. My intent to protect the native and the natural, and my sense of fairness in sharing and sharing alike the fruits of Mother Nature, is all one big human error in judgment. And I, in my arrogance to presume knowledge of and appreciation of ecology, have unwittingly become a minor player in a greater ecological drama that uses me for its purposes rather than I using it for mine.

Besides, who am I to institute the issues of territory and dominance for a species in which I do not even participate? Have I simply imagined I hear the jays screaming outside the perimeter of a pigeon horde, "There goes the neighborhood!?" Or do our visiting ringneck doves complain about their cousins who are by comparison late sleepers and late eaters? Do our cowbirds think in terms of settlers and pilgrims, indigenous and invaders, natives and immigrants?

Who owns the sky? Which feeding areas belong to which avians? I ask, but the feathered flyers are bewildered by my questions. From claiming a nesting place to competing for mates to canvassing an area for food, I have witnessed a mentality in birds rarely found among us "higher" life forms: they are gracious. Birds can struggle fiercely, then withdraw before violence occurs. They know how to wait their turn. They will try another area. They will tolerate the proximity of a wide range of relatives and non-relatives. They rotate leadership. They respect experience. They experience respect.

So what do I think I am teaching *them*?! What can I possibly contribute with my selective and high-minded killing to a social system that I secretly admire and envy? I am the more evolved, the more intelligent. I am biblically instructed and technologically able to exercise "dominion" over the garden of this planet. And I am embarrassed by my ineptness in the entire matter.

My analyst, C.J., our son's black lab, says that pigeons have come to represent for me all the people who have pushed me around in my life, and that on a cultural level, they are an image of my great embarrassment about my own marauding species, my own greedy and shameless brothers who honor war and territorial possession and murder and power and control. But Owen, our gray cat and my spiritual guide, says that the real drama is at an even more primitive level. He says that these beautiful and persistent birds are a reminder that I, in my moments of philosophical musing, demand too much of humanity, that I refuse to accept that we humans are indeed genetically predisposed to be greedy, warlike, territorial, possessive, controlling and murderous. He recommends that I start, not with forgiving pigeons, but with forgiving myself.

My wife, on the other hand, reads a lot. Her concern is about pigeon carcasses that get mixed with plastic-sealed garbage and instead of naturally decomposing in eighty days, remain largely intact for eighty years. She points out that my pellets, entombed in those bodies, will do their part in contaminating with toxic lead an otherwise healthy plot of landfill. And my rifle, she predicts, will eventually become a hot item in a garage sale; and it will be used to continue, probably indiscriminately, the demise of birds, squirrels, cats and windows.

Actually, I do not give much weight to a woman's opinion on these masculine matters. Nor do I listen to my analyst, nor am I particularly moved by the wise intentions of my spiritual director. Pondering deeply has taken the fun out of so many of my impulses and my plans. I am a man with a mission, a duty, a cause: pigeoncide.

But, it rained today. And I've had time to think. I may never finish my first box of pellets.

*Afterthought*    So. Is one man's pest another man's pet?

What happens when we think beyond our own back yard, beyond our immediate needs, and beyond our firmly held conclusions?

How do we respond to the gentle nudging that maybe we are not quite right, that the broader picture suggests not just a different answer, but a different question?

Can we see our own interests through the eyes of our neighbors and the other "co-owners" of the planet?

# *Neighbors*

*Forethought*  Prostitute. It's a word that hooks the mind into a clearly defined moral position, offers up a social ranking and predicts the eternal destination of the labeled woman (or man). We label so we don't have to deal with people as persons. Perhaps we fear that if "they" get too close, we might become confused about our solid moral and social position that nicely excludes "them" from the world of "us."

Our next author was surprised. He allowed one of "them" to get close, and his world was suddenly changed. He may never be the same.

South Main Street goes on for miles: fast food, convenience stores, small shopping "L"s, gas stations, motels, pawn shops, storage lots, liquor stores, auto parts. Whatever won't fit in the neater neighborhoods finds a home here. In fact, the very flavor of South Main is its generosity to all small businesses that together form the great economic and social barrier reef at the fringes of any large island of humanity, like Houston.

Anyone brave enough to stake a claim on the edges of this traffic artery, anyone strong enough to weather its noise and shale dust can turn a dollar, at least for awhile. For merchants are unforgiving here. There are no guarantees, no credit, and no one apologizes that a better deal can be

had somewhere else. Eat the fried chicken, or leave. All sales are final. Keep the traffic moving. Next!

Not that there is no integrity or pride among these entrepreneurs. There is, but of a more primitive kind. Here, trust is based on evidence of payment. Quality is based on familiarity with the product available. Price is a matter of convenience and time-saved. Satisfaction is less an issue of comparative shopping than it is accepting the context: if it's on the street, then it's a street service.

So it is with one of the more enterprising groups on the street, our ladies of the night, our sexual vendors, our proprietors of pleasure and distraction. Working as individual businesswomen, in partnerships, and in simple corporate structures, they are second-to-none in color and creativity in marketing their products. Availability of services is readily evident. Variety of packaging is entertaining and charming, if not necessarily convincing. And their aggressive style commands the respect of even those who disdain their presence.

This business enterprise weaves easily through the noisy atmosphere of South Main. It spreads throughout the length of roadside attractions, decorates it with laughter and light, and offers a friendly bantering among business people, customers, and passers by. They are not called *the* hookers, out there, apart from us, kept at bay so as not to contaminate our clean, upright, moral atmosphere. No, they are *our* hookers, right here, a part of us, claimed by us as integral members of our local business community and participants in the neighborhood. Our hookers know the street and its occupants like no other wandering group. They are our welcoming committee, helpful to the traveling confused, informed resources for local police patrols, and paradoxical beauty queens who add smiles to the otherwise bored faces of passersby.

Admittedly, I myself have gone through many attitudes and judgments about the business of prostitution. Disgust, fear, moral indignation, pity, irritation, sadness—I've had

these and probably other emotions. The way we view our
civic solicitors is largely a function of our state in life, our
age and experiences, and our sense of the fabric of real
people.

For however they are judged, first and foremost, these are
women. They are wives, mothers, daughters,
granddaughters, grandmothers, friends, sisters, aunts,
nieces and cousins. They are raising families, caring for ill
relatives, feeding drug habits, experimenting with fast
dollars, playing Russian roulette with their health, running
from someone or something. They are women. They live
next door to the president of the church volunteers, they
shop with the police chief's kids, they sit next to you in a
junior college biology class. Their children play with yours
on the school grounds. Here on South Main is where they
work. Usually they stand, holler, wave. Occasionally, they
approach a car entering or leaving a parking lot.

Tonight, as I drove home from having dinner with a
friend, a misty rain was gently soaking the city. My mind
was on fatigue, feeding the cats, sleep. And as I slowed to a
traffic light, I had not noticed a car to my left.

"Hey!"

I glanced into my rearview mirror, then to my left. There
she was, next car over, passenger side, signaling me to
lower my window. Obviously lost, needing directions.
Perhaps a friendly and alert sport about to warn me that I
had a low tire. Maybe an ex-client, someone who
remembered me from the office, a secret admirer. One of
my kids' friends—I can't keep up with all the names and
faces. Amazing how many speculations can whiz through
one's scanner in a mere flash. I politely complied and
lowered my side shield, letting the drizzle and the world slip
inside.

"Wanta party, honey?"

My scanner went on tilt. The buzzer went off. All guesses
wrong. And my ever-present split personality dashed

forward. My external self smiled and without hesitation, responded:

"No, thank you."

Clear, definitive, in charge. As for my internal self, I was a mass of confusion Where had she come from? Are they patrolling now? Did she want me? Was my car that attractive? Did she mean sex, drugs, sex and drugs, dancing, sharing a great book? Am I so obvious in looking starved for affection or excitement? Was my fly open?

Whatever puzzlements my internal self had were well protected, even saved by my cleverly trained, very mature external sounding, "No, thank you." But a coldness in the back of my neck revealed another level: fear. My God, what was I thanking her for? Her boldness? An invitation to a sordid motel, a proposed moral bullet through my loose brain? For identifying me as a weak, hungry, sexually perverted scumball of a man? For a chance at eternal damnation? Did my "thank you" prove the lie to my "no"? Had I exposed my vulnerability so foolishly?

"Are you sure?" she pursued, with a skeptical lilt and a sheepish grin.

Damn! I thought I had ended the interview. Hadn't I made myself perfectly clear? Or had I? A sinking feeling began to overtake my body and soul. Like a three-year-old with crumbs on his face, I now felt transparent. Had she seen something I had failed to conceal effectively? Did I not even know my own mind?

For millions of years, the fundamental premise of sanity has rested on the single presumption that a person knows that what he is thinking is in fact what he is thinking. When a child thinks she is thirsty and says so and is told that she is mistaken—that she only thinks she is thirsty and that she is only seeking attention—the first ripples of self-doubt, confusion, and eventual craziness begin to muddy her mind. She needs, even more than a drink, to know that her thirst is a valid statement of her current reality. For if thoughts and feelings are not accurate signals of our minds and bodies, then we lose that grip called sanity.

I didn't think I wanted to party. She, my night visitor, was now calling into question whether or not I was sure about my thoughts. She obviously had my best interest at heart—eager for me to know with certainty my wishes, my feelings, my motives. She had not fussed at me for my stubbornness. Nor had she expressed hurt, dismay, or anger at my declining her initial invitation, "Wanta party, honey?" She liked me, maybe even loved me as a fellow South Mainer. Had she not endearingly addressed me as "honey?"

It was I, not she, who was wondering about my initial decision of "no." Yet, her follow-up, "Are you sure?" had somehow touched a nerve deep inside. For I was struggling once again for a solid floor beneath me. My certainty was challenged, and my sense of who I was and what I was about was momentarily suspended in time and space. I was in effect told by this expert in her field:

"Go to your room, young man, and re-think what you have said, then come back to the table when you really know what you want!" "Go out into the hall, mister, until you are sure how to answer questions in this class!" "No, no, no sweetie: that's not what I want to hear. Think some more until you guess the right answer!"

Back to square one. I don't want to party. But am I sure I don't want to party? Yes! For heavensake I'm sure! But am I firm about my sureness, committed to my firmness, final on my commitment, sure about my finality? How many locks must I install before I know that the door is secure?

I did not want to party. That I was sure of. She did want to party. I held my ground. So did she. It was a wonderful moment of matched wits! A respectful sparring bout of neighbors meeting on a rainy night.

She congratulated me with a whimsical, "OK." She had the air of, "Your loss, sweetheart." And I responded with an equally respectful, "Have a good evening." Meaning, "Not me, but perhaps someone else."

Mercifully, the light changed, forcing me momentarily to attend to driving and rescuing me from further self-confusion. Her co-worker accelerated and their car passed on ahead. I watched them as a man supervises his neighbor's driving. Then their car slowed ahead as they pulled off on the road's shoulder, stopping beside a man standing in the rain. He leaned toward the car. As I passed by, I felt a slight pang of jealousy knife through my chest. My woman! After all we had together! Dumped for another man. Out of sight, out of mind. Right here on South Main.

*Afterthought*   So. When was the last time I let myself notice how I divide my world between "them" and "us"?

What things do I do, what words do I use, to reassure myself continually that I'm OK, but they're not so hot?

I know I have mixed feelings about a lot of moral and social issues. But do I allow myself to struggle with those conflicts? Or do I rigidly assume one position so as to avoid completely the struggle?

Is it OK for me to be unsure, to be unclear, to be undecided about issues that are apparently firm and clear for my friends?

# Because I'm Bigger, I'm Righter*

*Forethought*   No doubt about it. There are advantages to being the biggest kid on the block, the largest guy on the team, the tallest in the class. Size is power, power is intimidating, and intimidation can be immobilizing, unless the smaller of the group is resourceful with other talents like speed, wit, cleverness, flexibility, and humor.

Biology biases us to believe that bigger is better. Logic biases us to believe that being first is the same as ownership. Belief biases us into thinking that imagination is reality.

Danny questioned everything. And by questioning, he discovered that the great pecking order is highly arbitrary, controlled by words, and hung together by a fragile thread called seriousness.

He already knew he was late getting home. So as Danny Princette strolled across the open field in the dark, he began to rehearse explanations for his tardiness. The game lasted longer than he thought, the recent time change caught him

---

* Thanks to: *The Little Prince* by Antoine De Saint-Exupery.

off guard, Ms. Bartlett forgot he was upstairs with Tony. His mother had warned him about "stories" he used to avoid being held responsible for "dilly dallying," as she called it.

What a beautiful night it was. Even at age seven Danny had a keen sense of wonder for stars and moons and sunsets, along with his delight for frogs and worms and endless questions about the how's and why's of Nature. His father had once described him as an alien spy, intent on both acquiring all human knowledge and reducing to frustrated rubble the minds he tapped for his information.

Danny came to an abrupt halt halfway across the field. He scratched his nose nervously as he studied the unexpected and out of place scene: a man seated at a desk, grass all around, crickets chirping, only the light of the star-dusted sky above. His mother's awaiting eyes told him to avoid this curiosity and hurry home. His curiosity told him to glance away from his mother's eyes and investigate.

He approached the large desk, surveyed the large man seated behind it, and glanced at the large tablet on which he was writing. The man did not look up but said in a large voice.

"Yes?"

"Sir…"

"Yes?" still looking at his large tablet and writing.

"Sir, watcha doing?"

"Entries."

"What's that, Sir?"

"I am counting the stars up there and entering them in my ledger here."

"Why?" the boy asked.

"Look, young man! *I* am very important. I am counting the stars and entering them in my ledger. Therefore, they are *mine*. Now please run along."

Silence.

"Why?" began the boy again.

"Why, what?"

"Why are the stars *yours*?"

"Because *I* thought of it *first* to count them and list them here on my tablet. Therefore they are *mine*."

Silence.

"Sir…what is 'therefore'?"

"'Therefore' is 'therefore'! It means 'in conclusion'. It means that *because* of what stands or happens first, *then* what follows must follow. Because I count and record the stars, therefore in conclusion they are mine. Savvy?!"

"You mean you own the stars?!"

"Precisely."

"You mean you own the stars because you see them and count them and write down little numbers on your big tablet—that all of that together adds up to a *conclusion* that *therefore* you own the stars?"

"Couldn't have said it better myself. Now, beat it, and stop taking up my time with your endless questions."

Silence.

"Sir…?"

"What now?!"

"Do you own *time* also?"

"What are you talking about?"

"You said that I'm taking 'your time'. Do you also count time and record *it* too and *therefore* time also belongs to you?"

"Well…*yes*, as a matter of fact. It *is* my time, and I record it here in my watch on my wrist. *Therefore*, it is *my* time."

"Well, Sir," the boy brightened a bit with a smile, "do I own some time too?"

"Depends."

"Depends?"

"Yes. It depends on what you are *doing*. Are you doing something as *important* as counting and listing stars?"

"No, I don't think so." Frowning.

"Exactly! *Therefore* you are using *my* time because I *am* being *important*. And my time is important. And *therefore* and in *conclusion* I will thank you to stop bothering me in my important work!"

Silence.
"Why?"
The man ignored the boy.
"Why do you say *therefore* I am *bothering* you?"
"Because, one, I have important work to do. Two, you are
using *my* time to answer your questions, and three,
whenever someone takes me from my work during my time
I get distracted—I feel bothered."
"Oh, I see. A moment ago your conclusion was that I was
bothering you. Actually your conclusion is that *you* feel
bothered."
"It's the same!"
"Why?"
"Because I'm still bothered."
"But I was just asking questions. *Therefore* I was asking
questions. *Your* conclusion is different from mine."
"My conclusion is the *correct one!*"
"Why?"
"Because I thought of it *first*."
"Oh. And because we are talking on *your* time? In the
middle of *your* important work? That you are doing in your
*big* tablet on your *big* desk?"
"Yes…sorta."
"Oh, I see. Your *conclusion* about me is *more correct* than
mine because you and what you are doing are *bigger than I
am*!" Smiling sheepishly.
"Yes. Yes."
Silence. They looked cautiously at one another. The big
man laid his pen aside and propped his two chins on his two
clasped hands.
"Sir…"
"Why not. I can't get any work done anyway."
"Sir, when you say *therefore* or *in conclusion*, are you
making something *bigger* than it really is?"
"How so?"
"Well sir, when I ask *questions*, you make it *therefore* into
*bothering*. When you count stars, you make it *therefore* into

*owning* them. And when you make everything you do so *important*, then you make believe *in conclusion* that you are *more correct.* So when you make a *therefore* or a *conclusion*, then you are making what is happening seem *bigger* and *more important* and *more right* than it really is. Don't you think so?"

They stared at one another a long, long time.

"You know, kid, for someone so young, you think on your feet quite well. You do have a point. *Conclusions* are bigger than what they describe! *'Therefore'* does have a way of *adding* something that wasn't there before."

"Why do you have to *add something* to what is already there? Why can't you just *count* stars and I just *ask* questions? You don't really own the stars, and I'm not really bothering anyone. Those are just *added.*"

"There's a good reason for *adding* a *conclusion.*"

"There may be a reason. I'll ask whether it's good or not later!"

"Ha, ha, ha, ha, ha. You are a fast one, boy!"

They continued to laugh together.

The man continued. "The reason for *adding* a *conclusion* is that the *conclusion* makes one *feel better* about himself and what he's doing."

"You feel better about counting stars if you *conclude* that it's important?"

"Right."

"Don't you like to count stars?"

"Only if it's important."

"I like to count stars. But I have no *conclusion* that it's important."

"And do you *feel better* about yourself, kid, if it's not important work?"

"I've never thought of it before."

"My point, exactly! I feel better because I *conclude* that star-counting is important. *Therefore* I am *important* and I feel even *better.*"

"I feel good about star-counting."

"*Therefore*, because you just *feel good* and I *feel better*, I win!"

The man and the boy simultaneously collapsed in laughter, tears flowing from their eyes. A few moments of silence passed.

"I have to go now, Sir. Thank you for answering my questions."

"Thank you for asking."

Danny left and raced across the field. Reaching the back door steps of his house, he turned and glanced back toward the field. The porch light above him blocked his view, leaving the field in total darkness.

"And where have you been, young man?" he heard his mother's voice inquire from behind the screen door. Danny slowly faced his mother. He couldn't recall a single rehearsed story, so he risked the truth instead.

"You'll never believe what just happened, Mom."

"Probably not," she moaned, as she opened the door and let her young son inside.

*Afterthought*   So. And Therefore. And In Conclusion.

Aren't words wonderful?! Do we still know the difference between how we use words to convince and how we use words to hide, distract, derail, confuse, and deceive?

To what degree have we bought into our own importance? To what extent have we seduced ourselves into believing how indispensable we are to the company, to the group, to the family, to the world?

Can we still laugh at our arrogance, our rigidity, and our crushing logic?

Will we allow anyone to challenge our sense of who and what we are?

# My Membership Card

*Forethought*   People ask: what's your name, where are you from, where do you live, what work do you do, what's your political party, your religion, your social club? People ask these questions because we are largely defined by our membership in groups. We are who we are by whom we hang out with.

But how do we belong? What does it mean to be a member of an organization, a class, a club, a group? Sometimes we spend our lives in the same spot either in or out of groups. Sometimes we never learn how to join or how to enjoy participation with others.

Our next writer takes us on his adventure at trying to belong. And while we can chuckle at his attempts and failures, we secretly know we too have been there.

Ever since I can remember suffering from Low Self-Esteem, I knew I desperately wanted to be famous. I was eight when I actually realized I was nobody, so I must have been suffering from L.S.E. many years prior to that awakening. The neighborhood runt, last to be chosen on the teams, exiled from recurrent clubs, unable to keep up with the jocks, and ashamed to be seen with fellow filler-inners. Even in my family, I was referred to as *strungza*, a Sicilian euphemism for "turd."

MEMBERSHIP CARD

# SOMEBODY*

*EXACTLY *WHO* TO BE
DETERMINED LATER.

*J. M. Me!*
_____
CHAIRMAN/WOMAN/PERSON

Ignorance was bliss before eight. I just assumed that my life was supposed to be lived at the tail end of the alphabet. It seemed natural or normal or whatever that I would be holding one end of the rope while others got to jump. Somehow no one ever suggested or insisted that someday I would get a turn; I was so good at doing my job of making others look good.

"Hide and seek" was the epitome of my low life as a child. I never figured out how to get a turn at being It. Having become such an expert at blending in with the woodwork or foliage, I was so incredibly skilled at disappearing that I was never found. And by the time I surfaced to see where everyone was, they had grown tired of the game and had left.

Then came eight. No longer was I innocently odd-kid-out, but now I *knew* I was odd-kid-out. Before eight I at least had a role among my peers; now I had depression. I now knew hurt, anger, and impatience—all of which I probably had before but didn't know it.

And with this awareness came a gripping, growling wave inside of me. I no longer would stand being left out. I would not settle for just having my turn. Even being first would not quiet the storm of resentment filling my chest. I wanted to be in charge of the whole show!

At least, that's what I thought. The impulse of self-righteous indignation can hurl one into any number of directions.

My initial efforts at rising from the floor of insignificance were inspired by accident. On the occasion of a fourth-grade classmate's birthday party, I gave him a fairly well-wrapped box of corn flakes (it was all I could afford from my meager salary of pin-setting at the local bowling alley). The attendants laughed as Gil removed the gift wrap. I thought the gag was over. But convinced I had cleverly concealed his real gift in a corn flake box, he proceeded to tear open the box, exploding corn flakes into the next county. We all howled till we hurt. Whatshisname was a hit at the party with his silly gift. I took the credit, unplanned though the drama was, and set out to clown my way to popularity.

But humor, the safety net of our humdrum lives, is not the same as silly. I didn't know the difference. Humor fills, silly empties. Humor enriches, silly diminishes. Humor waits to be jarred loose, silly rushes in to perform, distract, and repeat itself. I took silly to be humor. Silly took me to the hot flash of public laughter and the lonely pit of the fool. "Do something funny!" was both my invitation to be noticed and my harsh lesson in social isolation. For once the clown act is over, the crowd has nothing to say or to give in return. Back to square one—invisible.

My next tactic was inspired by a recurring observation that "who's going first" was a much hated moment in the life of a group facing an uncertain task. I leapt at the opportunity. I would eat the fresh hot pepper to see if it was safe. I would do my book report first to break the class terror. I would sign the petition first to get the ball of protest rolling. I was a smashing success at going first and getting smashed first. I wondered if the pain was worth it. Pain is a wonderful teacher: it wore me down.

So my next strategy was more cleverly designed. If going first carried such a high cost, then perhaps there would be greater payoff in watching how things are done, then become better at it than anyone else. Sort of a best-on-the-team routine. But at what? No matter what I tried my hand at, I found I was out-run, out-spelled, out-dressed, out-dated, out-danced, and out-sung. I was out-biked, out-liked, out-played, out-paid, out-shouted, out-pouted, out-voted, and out-quoted. I performed fairly. Sometimes fairly well. Never the best of the bunch. I gave up.

But I learned something along the way of desperately wanting to be the best at something and always being bested—namely, that there was also someone judging how we all were doing. That someone in every group was the class critic, an alert observer and commentator on everyone else's performance. I could do that.

So I did. I studied the teacher's expectations, the Scout Oath and Law, the coach's instructions, the game rules, the Ten Commandments, correct form, traffic regulations, and proper etiquette. And I watched with the accuracy of a starving vulture how poorly my companions complied with or strayed from the (my) standard. I became referee, judge, critic, evaluator, advisor, consultant, and, ultimately, the self-appointed enforcer.

Unfortunately, my power and sense of esteem were short-lived. For after initially provoking respect and admiration from my friends, I later found them fearing, disdaining, and finally avoiding my comments—not to mention my presence. At best I was accepted as a non-participant critic; at worst I was still a non-participant.

I was also learning another gem: that the line between critic and cynic is only barely visible. I wanted it all not to matter. I found myself dismissing as irrelevant those people I most envied. I discredited those events I could not take part in. I demeaned those outcomes about which I was not invited to offer an opinion. I tried to convince them (and me) that it was all without meaning, knowing in the secrecy of my heart that the fundamental meaning was whether or not we shared an experience with someone—anyone—else. Back to the drawing board.

The truth does not initially set us free. Truth produces a wider range of awareness, awareness offers more options, options invite opportunity and rob us of excuses. With the death of excuses comes greater anxiety, confusion, and terror of loss of what we are accustomed to, which is why we avoid truth: it can get us lost.

My odyssey with the truth of belonging was more one of frustration than any other emotion. I was repeatedly bewildered by how what seemed to work for others kept escaping my grasp of effectiveness. It wasn't that I was failing to pay attention to good models, or failing to try out their finest qualities, or failing to alter my own approach. It was that I just kept failing. I couldn't find the right combination to fit into any target group.

So why not get help? Why not seek advice for my agony? Impossible. Things were never so clear during those early life experiences that would have allowed me the awareness that I was "in trouble". That was just my life. I never considered it any other way. That my life was a problem or that my failings deserved mention never crossed my frustrated and confused mind. What catfish knows he's in water? What elk, foraging in a blizzard for a few shoots of grass, considers his lot unusual? What child, having his nightly spanking for avoiding sleep, knows that he should file a complaint with the boss or seek the consultation of his colleagues?

And the few brief moments of faint objectivity I had that "something's rotten in Baytown" were never clear enough to allow me to formulate a personal statement of my dilemma. How could I ask help for what I could not define? Whom would I pick to complain to who would not be equally confounded by my vagueness? Not only was complaining not a highly prized behavior, but psychotherapy had not yet been invented.

I was mostly on my own. I say "mostly" because I still had my childhood walk-on heroes who lurked in the recesses of my memory: Tarzan, The Lone Ranger, and Jesus. My loyalty to them was untainted by my recurring mishaps. I knew they knew what I didn't know. They each had a secret of success, won acclaim through heroic deeds, and left lasting impressions on the crowds. Yet I saw equally well the downside of their lives: that no matter how much they each were loved, invited in, honored, and remembered; no matter how brilliant were their deeds or clever their strategies; no matter how much good they modeled—they always had to leave. They swung, rode, and rose to oblivion! Even they found no solace in the family, the clan, or the community. They could arrive, help, and depart, but staying was never their daily bread. Inclusion was never their reward. They never got a membership card.

I was determined to be an improved version of my three musketeers. Even if all my previous tactics failed, at least I could find a way to be in charge of others' lives to the extent that they would cherish my heroic skills and demand I remain a part of their lives. Rather than continue to struggle to be a crew member, I would become captain of the ship!

Where to start? At the top. How more critical to humankind's existence than to be mediator between people and God. I shall be a religious minister, I concluded. And in so doing, I would direct their souls for all eternity. By combining clerical studies with medicine, then specializing in psychiatry, I would corner the market on their spirit, body and mind. Graduate studies in law, politics, and economics would add power, wealth, and an international flavor to my importance in the lives of the populations at large. Having a family of my own would model for everyone the epitome of love, companionship, positive parenting and solid community building. And I would do it all without uttering a single scream, firing a single shot, or dying a singular death.

Such was the grandiosity of my imagination. And no, I never seriously attempted to fill the slot of Earth Consulate/God Assistant. But when one thirsts for significance, equates power with esteem, and views position as inclusion, then there is no end to one's potential madness for membership. When a child misses out on learning those social skills of participation, sharing, and celebration, then he is left (out) to discover compensatory ways to feel relevant to his fellow humans.

By going through the experiential list of supporter, clown, expert, coach, critic, cynic and finally C.E.O., I learned ever so painfully that none of these roles satisfies the yearning to be a member. For paradoxically, each task set me apart from the group rather than grant me the grace of feeling a part of it. My individuality continued to overpower my sense of collective inclusion.

On occasion of a group activity—a religious celebration, a professional meeting, a funeral, a conference—I would deliberately fold myself into the crowd, become one among a dozen or hundred, to re-discover what I have historically struggled against. I became invisible, swallowed up in an ocean of faces. The crushing sense of insignificance destroyed even my slightest effort at feeling included or wanted. For I knew in those regressive moments that what I wanted was not simply inclusion, but recognizable, impactful, relevant, significant membership. Not a cog, but a character; not a number, but a name; not a face, but a fellow.

Inclusion as a member is not so easily defined as we think, particularly if it can be defined with an almost infinite range of experiences by people. If it's ever defined at all. Which I doubt. Membership is one of those elusive thoughts, wishes, feelings, or intuitions that we rather assume or snuggle up to or shy away from without ever quite noting what *It* is that we are dealing with. So rather than focusing clearly on what we prefer and set out working to achieve it, we rather massage the whole issue of membership like a wad of dough, and settle lazily for some external symbol that represents infusion in the club. A uniform, a flag, a meeting hall, a series of rituals, a pendant, a ring, an official membership card with my very own name and renewal date clearly typed or embossed thereon. What could be more definitive and reassuring of the fact that I belong?

Unfortunately, these symbols don't quite do it either. For each of us carries a secret inside, namely, that the sorority emblem on the wall is *not* the group's experience, no more than a letter jacket is the band's experience, no more than a photo is the event. I have never seen a whale, though I belong to its dedicated group of preservers. I carry a national membership card of my profession, though I have yet to attend a local or state or regional conference. And the indelible baptismal mark on my soul has yet to endow me with the experience of being Christian.

What is it that I am supposed to feel when I pledge allegiance to the flag of the United States of America and to the Republic for which it stands? What does it mean to be called Italian or Australian or Russian or Southerner or Texan or Bostonian or Union or doctor or civil servant? Or for that matter, how do I even experience my membership in my own families?

Before we fear physical death, we fear two forms of a living death: inclusion to the point of becoming anonymous, and exclusion to the point of becoming anonymous. Not to matter inside, not to matter outside. We rage against either, we jockey for recognition in hope of avoiding both.

I've tried it all. I've worn the uniform, attended the meetings, worked for advanced placement, carried my membership card, walked in the marches, shouted at the rallies, wrote articles for the journal, stood to be counted. And I moved from one job and role in my groups to other jobs and roles in my groups, searching always to answer the questions: "Am I in or out?" "Do I fit or not?" "Is this what belonging is about?"

My answer, as of this century, is this: I belong mostly when I am actively involved with my fellow members, but I dare not let my stay be long. The group, any group, is highly transitional, largely fabricated, mostly functional. It is not my whole life, my total self-definition, my end all. For there are times when I want to attend, and there are times when I just want to have been invited—without having to attend. There are moments when I just want to follow, and there are moments when I am bewildered by why I wasn't asked to take charge.

No one task of group supporter, judge, leader, or clown is to be held onto with tenacity. They are each appropriate at different moments in my participation as a member. What works today will be inappropriate tomorrow. What earned me respect among my peers at yesterday's event, will likely shame me at today's meeting should I press for continuity of my behavior and skill.

As low man on the totem pole in my youth, I thought I wanted to be on top. I have come full circle. Having experienced every position on the pole, I now know that my issue is not the position, but the flexibility and freedom to try them all.

Oh, the power of the top.

Oh, the freedom of the bottom.


*Afterthought*   So. How do we belong to someone or some group?

What is the list of things available to us that create participation in any group—starting with "showing up"?

Why is membership in group activity easier for some of us men than it is for others?

What do we repeatedly do to avoid opportunities to join in and enjoy the groups available to us?

What conclusions have we drawn about ourselves that discourage people from inviting us to participate with them?

# Men Are
# No Damn Good!

*Forethought*   How reliable is our memory? Our childhood days and the people we knew back then are clearly recorded, sorted, and stored in easily retrievable mental files. Right?

Not hardly! We piece it together as we go along. And some things, like who Dad really was and what sort of woman was Mom, are sometimes the hardest data to get ahold of.

Try this one on for size: recall how you learned to be a man or a woman. Trust me: it did not come automatically. When Carl set out to put together the pieces of his "on becoming a man" story, he was caught up in a tangle of good and bad, male and female, confusion and humor.

Let's follow his journey…

Remembering one's past is a very creative process. We do not remember facts—those highly sought-after, indisputable trophies of objective data that supposedly lie beyond the realm of personal bias, opinion, and passion. Facts are slippery little devils. Now you have them, now you don't. We crave hard facts for conviction, for direction, for ordering

our lives. We need to know that a dollar is worth a dollar, that my chair won't move out from under me as I sit, that "no" means "no," that our past does in fact precede our present. Yet none of these are hard facts. They exist by mutual agreement among a limited number of people who get through the day a bit easier by keeping to this agreement.

Remembering is a current act of reconstructing a personal experience. It is a quick trip back (usually?) in time, along a path of a single emotion, sound, color, smell, taste or whatever trigger sets off the adventure. And the scene that we arrive at is less like a movie or a photograph (hard data?!) and more like a collage or puzzle of poorly fitting pieces. The central creative act occurs when we jam the pieces together to form a definitive scene. For the human mind craves definition.

After shoving the puzzle pieces together to form a scene, the next creative act is to endow the scene with meaning—a personal interpretation that adds to and supports one's world view, community role, family position, and personal philosophy. Then follows the telling or sharing of this memory, a social component of this creative act that adds further color and drama to the scene. And finally, there is the re-telling and re-telling of the memory, adding personal conviction and historical solidity to the recall.

But did *it* happen back then? How much of the puzzle picture is true? What part is embellishment? Does it matter, and why? What humor! Are our lives built on the solid blocks of recordable and verifiable facts; or is the fabric of meaning, value, cause and outcome the result of a well-disguised process of art: the creation of self? What drama!

With these questions in mind, a story begins.

The trigger is a carpet pattern: a broken arch of gold against a reddish-maroon background, swirls of flowers at the base of the arch. It is 1946, maybe '47, and my six-year-old heart is pounding against my ribs. The carpet pattern becomes blurred as my eyes fill with tears. And inside or outside my head, I hear my mother's scathing instruction:

"Just go ahead and undress here in the front room, Carl, and then get on the couch. Don't be fussy about it. You don't have anything anybody wants to see."

Dizziness and nausea enveloped me like a large pillow slip. And even though vomiting might have given me an excuse to escape to the bathroom, I knew it would only make matters worse. I would have to clean up the vomit, then be harassed for being a baby—again. Not worth it.

So glancing embarrassingly about at my two younger girl cousins, I slowly peeled. My eyes were glued to the golden arches, my mind counting one, two, three, four, five— hoping I would not run out of numbers before I disappeared under the blanket on the couch. I hated that my underwear was more like my cousins' than the boxer shorts my uncle wore. I felt cursed, probably neutered—had I known the term. I was drenched in confusion.

The puzzle piece fades. And the trigger of confusion reaches for a vague summary of memories. I had been raised by a hard-working and reportedly devoted woman. Devoted to what was never quite clear to me. I knew it was not devotion to my father whom she dumped soon after I was born, nor to a particular apartment or house that seemed to change every year or so, nor to even her own extended family about whom she complained regularly. She testified that she lived for her two sons, me and my older brother, Jim. Yet neither of us felt her devotion as much as we felt her sense of labored responsibility, impatience, rage, and a determination to prove her maternal heroism to everyone around (herself?). And to add a touch of tragic humor, she had named each of us after husbands that she had hated and promptly divorced. Confusion.

What we two guys felt but did not at all understand was that somehow we were the wrong kids. Or we were the wrong version of kids that our mother probably never intended to have in the first place. We were at least the wrong sex. For the curse we heard chanted time and time again by our duty-bound mother was: "Men are no damn good!" And that will bewilder any child.

The puzzle piece fades, and bewilderment pushes me toward reflection. How does a boy child make sense out of that sexual expletive of his own mother? Here he is, standing before his second grade class at show-and-tell time:

"My mother did it with my daddy, that she hates, because they are no damn good. And I was born, and named after him, and she says she loves me anyway. My mother never talks about me growing up to be a man someday, which she hates. I don't know why I don't trust her."

Not only is half the human race deleted as unacceptable to the good half, but we boys find ourselves trapped in the bad half. Mother struts about proclaiming her disassociation from all males, yet fails to notice that her beloved offspring are in fact diminutive versions of the hated sex.

A unique dilemma? Not really. History is filled with stories of how frail, limited, misplaced, and mismarked humans have survived in the midst of overwhelming confusion and contradiction. Cripples have become great athletes, orphans have brought pride to their adoptive parents, seeming idiots proved to be geniuses, the lowly have become leaders. For it is in the wiring of the human soul both to make some meaning out of a confusing world and to carve out a destiny that justifies that meaning. As the philosopher Plutonius once said:

"Show me a day in the life of a man, and I will show you the beliefs he creates in order to get through it."

So also did we two sons make sense out of our curse of maleness. Jim proved to be the more clever. He would eventually take the road of becoming our mother's worst nightmare—a typical bad boy and prototype of a no-good man. He quickly cornered the market on being a rascal, disinterested in school, tough, skilled in sports and sport statistics, obsessed with dirt, marbles, cars, and, finally, girls. I've never forgiven him for his single-minded genius.

I was not so bright a fish as my brother, for the seriousness of our mother's words had hooked me, and hooked me badly. I felt abandoned by my brother; I stood alone in my confusion. I was fairly sure I was not a girl, although the secret wish had on occasion crossed my mind. I knew I would never become a woman. But whereas other males could rely on a base line of "boy-ness" and proceed from there to "man-ness", my position was not that clear. Unlike Jim, I feared our mother's disapproval, I wanted her well-guarded love, I needed inclusion in our family, I yearned for peace of mind and the semblance of self-confidence. She owned all this and would loan it to me now and then if only I could stumble upon the secret of winning her smile of approval.

Jim, the rat, had stolen the slot of boy; I would somehow have to create the category of atypical non-male. I would not become female, nor would I become gay by default. I would carve out a picture of myself as *not*: definitely not female, and decidedly not male. It was sheer intuition, not a matter of mental gymnastics.

One thing I had going for me was that I was growing up in the '40s and '50s, not in the '80s and '90s. Sexual abuse, sexism, victimization, recovery, and dysfunctional families had not yet been marketed. So I did not feel crushed and maimed. Nor would I resort to the law for relief (read "revenge") or compensation (read "security"). What I felt were confusion and frustration. What I thought was: "Somehow I will make this work." What I did was invent myself in a world that offered no model.

The puzzle piece slowly fades, and the word "invent" now takes hold of my memory.

A veritable avalanche of snapshots competes for my memory file. I listened to my mother, aunts, and older cousins discuss the despicable traits of men in their lives. And with each description I formulated and recorded on a small spiral tablet in my brain what I would have to become in order not to be like my unacceptable uncles, grandfather, ex-fathers.

Men smoked, told dirty jokes, scratched their crotches.

I jotted down: don't smoke, only listen to dirty jokes, scratch only from the depth of my pants pockets.

Men drink, they're unreliable, and lazy around the house.

I would swear off all alcohol except my grandpa's wine he gave me. I would make no promises. And I would become the best housekeeper in the neighborhood.

Men were always competing, were preoccupied with sex, and they were hairy. Now the list was getting harder, and my *not* resolves tougher. I won't play ball to win: I'll pretend it's just for fun. I'll find a way never to be sexual. Maybe become a nun. No, a priest. And when my face breaks out with a disgusting layer of whiskers, I will pull them out by the roots with tweezers—just as the Native Americans did with clam shells.

What confused me about this piece of the puzzle was that while I was negating as much maleness as I could identify, I was beginning to have mixed feelings about what I admired in women. They were hard workers, effective in family affairs, able to mingle and talk at a single bound. Prayerful, spiritual, loving, creative were the attributes of women. But I didn't trust women. They made men look small and immature by comparison, though I rarely heard them openly demean men as my mother did. Could my mother possibly be right, or was her vision limited to only those limited men inside her limited world?

The term "inside" changes the scene, and a new puzzle piece slips into memory. For the years that stretched from childhood through adolescence, I actively searched outside my family for men who could bring some hope to my now emerging despair about being a boy, and later, a young man. I had P.E. teachers in elementary school who were unimpressed with my small size and passive, playful attitude toward sports. In the fifth grade my only male teacher found me impertinent and disposable because of my insistence that nine times zero equaled not zero but nine zeros. And in the eighth grade my mechanical drawing teacher had a beard, for heaven's sake! And my high school coaches smelled like men.

Then a new wrinkle entered my odyssey. It began to dawn on me that perhaps it was not the world of men that was so disappointing. Maybe it was my own research through negation. Was there, pray tell, a scratch on the lens through which I was viewing the men around me? I speculated that I just might be caught in my own mother-assisted, self-constructed web of male criticism, spotting the predictable flaw in every man I encountered. I was perchance re-affirming my belief—no, my mother's belief—that men were no damn good. No decent man had a chance. They would all be smashed by my (her?) critical red pencil. And my disappointment in them slowly became an almost uncontrollable rage at her.

But by now, the die had been cast: I was compelled to disprove what I had been enjoined by my mother to believe. I was hopelessly searching for one or two truly good men in Sodom who could pass the test of my mother's vengeful sword of male annihilation. I found none. The city would have to be torched with my rageful disappointment and humiliating failure.

I wandered in a daze for two or three years, going through the motions of high school, family, church, and friends. I so wanted to prove my mother wrong; I wanted more to trap her into finally approving of me as a good man. That was when I was inspired, sitting beside the city canal, to make my final assault: I would become a perfect man.

Unlike saints before me who had dedicated their lives to saving others and preaching the gospels, I was resolved to eliminate every flaw of my manhood. In so doing, I would save my mother from her self-imposed loneliness and rage, and I would win God's (Mom's) blessing for a life of purified and decaffeinated maleness. As a bonus, I would become the pace-setter so needed by half the population of the world and coincidentally the envy of the other, supposedly better, half.

My inspirational puzzle piece lay on the card table of my mind while a succession of others fell around it. For what followed that adolescent dream could fill the pages of the most boring novel of the century. Let it just be said, briefly, that I failed, slowly at first, then later with a crashing series of blunders. I sought out and hid inside a new couch blanket, the church. She proved to be schizophrenic, torn between theory and practice. Besides, how could I sit comfortably with an institution referred to as Holy Mother. A contradiction if I ever felt one!

My asthmatic lungs robbed me of the chance to credit my willpower with never smoking. But I lied and took the credit anyway. I was obsessed with food, wine, haircuts, boots, and totally destroying an enemy on the tennis court. Try as I could not to see, smell, listen to, or touch women, my early adulthood was littered with sexual fantasies, close dancing, dreams of passion, yearning and fearing romance, and a ceaseless stirring of emotions between my bellybutton and my knees.

Before my very eyes, my life was unraveling as a great mass of contradictions. For strive as I did to reach the mountain top of "I thank you, Lord, that I am not like the rest of men," I was in fact being hurled into the throes of becoming very much like the rest of men. Yes, the ladies were drawn to me, counted me among their confidants, admired my show of strength, virtue, and disdain for all that was macho. But I remained unchosen as a lover. My lust for admiration separated me too far from my lust for skin. I wanted to be held. They wanted my support. I finally understood the curse of the hero: honored and alone. I had become my worst nightmare: I had become my mother.

Loneliness and rage, my frequent bedfellows, were now forming a clear puzzle piece. For the harder I worked to perfect myself, the more like a lost sheep I became. The stronger I fought to make myself indispensable to someone, the more rejection I discovered. And the more lonely I walked the streets of my life, the more visible my rage.

I raged at the world around me for being so cruel and disappointing. I raged at my most visible target—mother—for so cruelly cursing me with the unachievable damn good man I could never quite be. And, each time I passed a mirror, I raged at myself for falling into her/my trap in the first place, then failing to crawl out in the second place. From the altar of marriage to the courtroom of divorce I raged at a wife for failing to be what my mother never was—a woman who would approve of me in spite of my afflictions of maleness. I raged at an unreliable God, then at my disappointingly imperfect children, my unfair boss at work, my utter mockery of a life. I lived a decade of humiliating, despairing rage. How my family survived me, I will never know.

Darkness.

A new scene, broken and vague, now forms another puzzle piece. With a slight headache from too much apple wine the night before, I sat at the back of a church early one Sunday morning. I was not there to worship or to pray, and much less to be in a crowd for Mass. I was there to think about my fatigue. I was tired of the struggle. An old friend, The New Testament, sat in the hymnal shelf in front of me. Impulsively I took it out, and, opening it to St. Matthew's contribution, I read an utterly unfamiliar translation:

"Be exactly what you are, just as your Father who lives in eternal peace is exactly what He is." I was stunned, for that very passage had always been rendered as:

"Be ye perfect, as your heavenly Father is perfect."

"Perfect" I had tried and found wanting. But "exactly what you are" had a different ring to it. I felt that familiar rush of excitement, just behind my breastbone, my signal that I had stumbled upon a hidden treasure I wanted to share with whomever was nearby. I looked around. I was alone in this religious cavern.

So I sat still, remained silent, and listened to the flow of thoughts crowding in for attention. "If I am a frog, then my destiny is to be the particular frog that I am, not the jumper sitting over there on that lily pad. But I am not frog. I am human, and each of us is by definition not duplicable, imperfect, flawed, broken, limited. So to be just human is to claim, love, and share my imperfect nature, to love others because they too are perfectly imperfect, and to allow them to love me because I am also imperfect. I am good, not in spite of my flaws, but *because* of my flaws." Mother would not be pleased.

An awakening was taking place, a rebirth, a renewal. It was grander than insight. It was a re-shuffling of the same deck of cards in my life and discovering that 3s, 4s, and 6s are no longer throwaways but keepers, that they are the cards that make the queens and kings look good.

The final piece in the puzzle was the walk from church to my apartment that early morning. Hands in pockets, vision blurred, I surveyed some implications of that singular reading. Beauty, skill, competence, brilliance and rank that I found in others I could admire and envy—even consume. But crankiness, hurt, meanness, impatience, clumsiness, and despair were my invitations to come close, to love, to nurture. I began to realize that others' imperfections and their impact on me are what elicited my love.

Likewise my own efforts to be the perfect man, to compete, to crush, to be only the best resulted in my being admired, even worshipped. Such emptiness and loneliness! But my hurt, my anger, my frustration, my obsession with chores, my critical nature, my clumsiness, and my fears were the windows of my soul that provoked either revulsion or endearment among my fellow humans. My flaws were the bridge that some chose to cross and love me for.

I felt that by choosing to be exactly who and what I was, I simultaneously was taking charge of my life for the first time. This transformation was not only the shedding of a dry, hard, and imprisoning skin of obsessional escape from maleness; but it was also a final separation from an unsatisfiable mother whom I had let hold me in the grip of a love-hate expectation that I be for her what no man had been or could be—perfect, and damn good.

In effect, I was letting go of my *own* grip on her, her promise of approval, my insane search for perfection. And most importantly, I was letting go of my own rage at the comic tragedy I was living out before a bemused God and among my bewildered friends.

I had spent the first forty years of my life confusing maleness with badness, approval with love, perfection with goodness. I had seen human imperfections as flaws to be ashamed of and apologized for, blemishes that required a lifetime of effort to eradicate from the intended pure fabric of our humanity. I had used my critical skills to blame every man as a disappointment and condemn every woman as a liar. And I did it all wearing the costume of a hero.

My own odyssey to become first an unmale, and then a perfect man ended in the rubble of a caricature. I had become a lifeless puppet, held up by the fragile strings of accommodation, image, approval and fear. When I finally cut those strings and risked the brief terror of free-fall, I landed on strong and imperfect (flat)feet, breathed with healthy and imperfect lungs, looked with clear and imperfect eyes, and loved with a passionate and imperfect heart.

Mother was right: men are no damn good. Men are also no damn bad. They are, when they finally wake up, beyond the judgment of good or bad. They are men.

*Afterthought*  So. Ever notice that we recall the past in such a way that the "facts" support the story we have already told ourselves?

We know who we are by the *conclusions* we have drawn about our past events and past experiences. What sort of men would we be today if we had understood those events differently?

Does our maleness or femaleness still depend on our doing the same "proofs" of our sexuality as when we were younger?

How has our sexual definition softened or expanded as we have grown older?

Who is our current model of being a mature man today?

# *Pop Quiz*

*Forethought*    Let's shift gears and slide into one of those more colorful events in a man's life—fatherhood. It begins with the choking dread of twenty-five years of responsibility and ends with the gasping awareness that a quarter century was greatly underestimated. We dodge it, deny it, even hide from being Dad; but the kids keep showing up. They don't go away!

With the following essay, we start in the middle. Dad finds himself cornered by his adolescent daughter in a public arena from which there is no escape unless a meteor slams immediately into earth. And he learns an important lesson again: kids are always one jump ahead of their parents.

Children should be seen and not heard. My parents regularly chanted this slogan, especially in moments of our greatest curiosity or their most monopolizing conversations. Whether I ever fully respected the injunction, I can't recall. What is clear is that I hated it, vowing privately that should I ever have children, they would never suffer the frustration and silent rage of having cotton stuffed in their mouths. I would do it differently.

So I did. Among other parenting strategies that seemed good ideas, I encouraged (or at least allowed) our children to have access to the airways of adult conversation. They were free to ask, challenge, object and initiate—bowing only to an occasional instruction to take turns. What we, the enlightened mom and dad, failed to anticipate was their own creative delight in bringing up subjects of a provocative nature, especially in family gatherings: "Why do big people have more rights than little people?" "Dad gets to holler, but not us kids!" "My underwear crawls!" Adamant food preferences, their selection of friends, clothes, and jokes—all was grist for the verbal mill. Mom and dad could be counted on to hear, include, respond, even if this included an occasional gag, cringe, or bit lip. No reprisals for talk.

Until adolescence, that is. For what we consider cute, precocious, and entertaining at seven is in the behavior of a fifteen-year-old nothing short of irritating disrespect and grounds for justifiable "teenicide." Their daring and risking and pushing against my parental stamina eventually became my daily migraine and my constant fear.

And that memorable day at Chico's restaurant will be forever a summary of this tug of war. I sat reading the menu. My fourteen-year-old daughter and her best friend sat across, giggling over a private joke or a piece of gossip, practicing both being seen and being heard. I was hardly listening. Surrounding us sat dozens of taco and nacho junkies at tables so close our chairs occasionally interlocked. The noise was too loud for comfort, yet loud enough for some semblance of privacy. A finger appeared at the top of my menu, gently lowered it. My daughter's eyes met mine.

"Pop, can I ask you a question?"

From past experience, I recognized this line as the verbal equivalent of the click made by a .38 revolver being cocked for firing. What's the setup this time? A rare and genuine request for information? Naah. A check for credibility, an inquiry to find out if Dad can tell the truth about something she already knows with certainty? Maybe. An invitation to affirm a thought or feeling that she feels uneasy to claim?

Sometimes. A trap in which to expose the laughable limitations of her old-fashioned parent and a public arena in which to smash him? My heart sank as I braced, then dodged:

"Yes, you can have chili con queso, too."

"Thanks, but the question is: When do you think someone should start having sex?"

It was a perfect hit, broadside. The seven tables surrounding us fell silent. E. F. Hutton could not have been more successful at immobilizing a crowd. I swallowed hard, smiled. And in one-eighth of a second, my entire parental understructure collapsed.

These are golden moments. Correction: these are hot lead moments. No retreat, no script. Nothing but that naked next moment in the public eye. The mind races for a clue, a starting point, a fix, *something*, for God's sake.

The one-eighth second now expanded to minutes. I was flying blind. All instruments spun wildly on the front panel. My wing tips struggled for balance, my fuel pouring from its storage tanks. And below—the bleakness of a jungle floor rushing hungrily up to devour me like a frog tracking a crippled dragonfly.

I chanced a glance to my left. An array of schoolteachers sat poised with red pencils and sneering smiles. Now to my right. Six police officers, plainclothesmen for concealment, were already reaching for cuffs and clubs. And toward the rear of this smoke-filled entrapment sat a panel of three judges, ready to sentence me as quickly as my response was about to convict me.

Hours passed. My child, my little girl, my darling, my obnoxious adolescent, my executioner sat with eyes glued to mine as her hand deliciously fingered the trap door lever that would send me helplessly into the abyss of shameful exposure to the world.

Dazed and sweating (I never sweat!) my mind scanned for help. At some primitive level I raged at being once more held hostage by a pop quiz. I have lived in utter terror of the sudden, unanticipated question. I have despised that terrible, recurring land-mine of surprise inquiry, that posture of total and irretrievable dread when I'm called upon to recite, report, review, recount, list, or define. And I go blank. Not just blank, but bottomless, black, crushing, screaming blank. Inside I struggle with philosophical cries:

"Why me?!" "Why now?!" "Not fair!"

Memories of absurd responses race past me. In the fourth grade, Ms. Thatcher asked unannounced, "What do beavers make?" And since mine was the only hand not waving, I was culled out for martyrdom. In my panic and complete mind-empty fashion, I responded with a meek: "Baby beavers?" My first recall of how sheer horror could be misinterpreted as sarcastic humor.

At sixteen while walking home late at night, I was stopped by our men in blue and asked to identify myself. I stood dumbfounded and confused. Unable to recall any of my three names, I hurriedly reached for my school I.D. stowed in my wallet. What happened next is still a blur. Car doors slammed, revolvers flashed, orders screamed, hands up, feet spread! My name, for Pete's sake, what is my name?! My first memory of how frozen stupor was read as criminal intent.

Or last month, as I was introducing my sweetheart to a friend. "Michael, this is...." Blank. A self-imposed quiz of "Guess the right name." Same outcome. And this, my most recent experience of how poor recall can be judged as careless, insensitive, and cruel embarrassment for those you love.

My one-eighth second, now a three-week pause, was shattered as my adolescent accuser spoke.

"Pop..."

She was holding her ground. Had she been a more merciful teenager—scratch that: "merciful" and "teenager" are contradictory when directed simultaneously at the jugular of an elder. She was solidly adolescent, and she held me in her stare like a cat sizing up a cornered mouse.

Then the miracle occurred. It was a miracle that has left an indelible imprint on my soul, one which has served me well when all else has failed in the face of a surprise attack. It was stroke of genius, not generated by me but placed there as a gift by a passing spirit who must have suffered more than I. It entered me suddenly, filled my lungs, stretched my vocal cords, moved my lips. And as I yielded to the spirit's authority, it forced me to respond:

"You're asking the wrong question." Incredible! An escape hatch I could never have stumbled onto myself. I quickly claimed it as my own, plagiarizing as I had never done before or since.

"Yes," I now smugly continued. "There's something about your question that needs revising." I was awash in arrogant security. My body began to reconstitute itself. I felt the chair under me again.

"Then what's the right question?" she shot back, half sarcastic, half teasing. She knew darn well that she had created this drama, directed it, and was starring in it. She was now acutely aware of the audience waiting on the edges of their chairs. Hers and mine were the only sounds on stage.

I scanned the original question. I was now on a roll. My spiritual jump start had the old machinery moving again.

"The issue, Madame, is not when you start having sex, but what kind of friendship you have that calls for a sexual expression."

The crowd went crazy with applause and shouting. Cameras flashed. A band struck up a circus tune. My daughter and her friend laughed approvingly. I was ecstatic, not because I was brilliant in my (the spirit's) response but because the meat hook was no longer lodged in my left lung. I could breathe again. I could remember my home address. My brain had returned from its float trip to its usual underground cave back to my head. I, the dunce, had regained my footing.

We bantered, we sparred, we wrestled the topic down to the mat, each of us gaining a hold, then slipping away. A good struggle.

I truly cannot remember the details of the conversation. I can only recall with warmth and some pain the agonizing moment of "gotcha!" that had sprung from its hiding place and snared me again. There have been times when I have dreamed of reading and memorizing the entire revised Encyclopedia Britannica, of devouring the now-in-print 684 books on trivia, of having twenty-four hours uninterrupted access to the central library resource phone, of, of.... It wouldn't help. There is no keeping up, no staying informed, no perfect readiness. My Boy Scout motto of "Be Prepared" failed me then and fails me to this day.

My faith no longer lies in being ready. My faith lies instead in being open—open not only to the unpredictable next moment, the recurring surprise, but even more, open to whichever wandering angel might again pass my frozen and gear-locked mind, touch it with a drop of warm oil, then gracefully pretend with me that the thought was mine all along.

*Afterthought*  So. Did our generation of parents commit a fatal mistake by inviting our kids to speak their minds and challenge ours?

What do we do when our children present us with a personal question for which we have no rehearsed answer? Deflect? Reflect black? Play stupid? Attack? Wonder?

Do we have the presence of mind to wonder what is really being asked beyond the literal question:

- an inquiry about us, the Dads!?
- a wonderment about the questioning child?
- a test for credibility?

Why do we so fear being discovered as not all-knowing, not always prepared, not having the right solution?

# *Family Fights*

*Forethought*    Children grow up, mature, leave home, start their own careers and families, and return on holidays to celebrate the success of their family history. Such is the fantasy of the mentally structured male-turned-parent. In human existence of the past ten thousand years, there is evidence of only eleven children who actually made such a smooth transition.

Most Dads discover, much to their chagrin, that another phenomenon pervades and slows down the timely emptying of the family nest: kids keep fighting. Dads keep breaking up the fights, give Lecture 423 on mutual rights and respect, threaten premature abandonment, bribe their ex-wives to reclaim full and perpetual custody.

Our next author, a single parent, just wanted a memorable vacation with his grown children. What he got was an opportunity to wonder, perhaps for the first time, why they fought.

At the outset, it seemed like a simple and fun-filled idea: Dad and two kids will go skiing together for five days in beautiful Colorado. A condo for four would give them space to sprawl around. "Swooshing" down the mountain in billows of snow would award them ample individual and family activity, fun and happy memories. Evenings would be

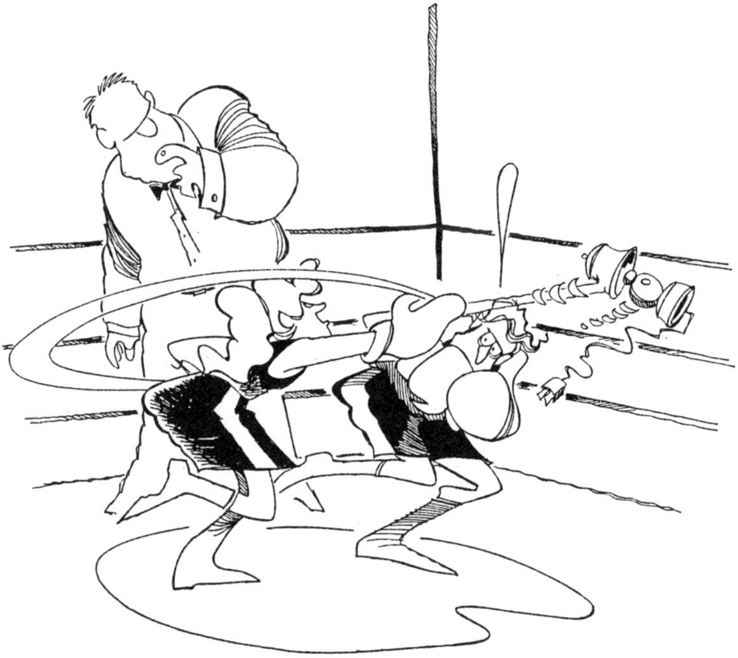

magically taken with dining out as they joyfully reviewed the day's adventures. Simple enough.

But Mother Nature and her husband, God, in their infinite humor, had other ideas, other schemes, other lessons to teach these three innocents. Yes—there's always something to learn or re-learn from what looks like simple, sweet dreams. No matter how well-planned, how well-intended, it is the unexpected that presents our most powerful moments of insight, frustration, and humility. The unanticipated remains our most precious invitation to call us out of our smugness about how much we know and how well we are doing.

To the casual observer, as well as to the casual observance of the three grownups themselves, this would be the fifth ski trip of a successful father and his college-aged offspring, now living apart, all healthy, all excited about the reunion adventure.

So what had they *not* planned on? They had, as every family does by definition, omitted the obvious: they were a family. They had failed to pay due respect to one of the most powerful forces in the universe: any group of two or more people who grow up together (even for a brief period) and constitute that fascinating collective called a "family" will, whenever they come together, re-constitute that family in all of its joy, hatred, successes, failures, alliances, fights, politics, behaviors, emotions, and beliefs.

It cannot be otherwise. And what is fascinating is that the family thus constituted maintains a kind of stubborn life all its own, in spite of the efforts of each member to make it otherwise.

The three of them knew one another's vulnerabilities. They had a level of openness and safety wherein they could talk about those soft spots and hard points, even laugh and joke about them. They could tell wonderful stories about Dad's loudness when enraged, Son's provocativeness, Daughter's uncanny ability to make any event a major production. Part of the beauty of their on-going family history was their hard-won ability to hold this history in their hands and share it easily and humorously.

Then they got a little cocky. They forgot, as any family does, that given a circumstance or event that catches them off-guard, disrupts their agreed-upon agenda, displeases or disappoints one of its members, they are hurled instantly and unavoidably back into their very own history that now holds *them* in *its* tight hand. The tide is suddenly reversed, and instead of them living it and recalling it, their history now dictates their responses, their emotions, and their conclusions, from which they, for the moment, cannot disentangle.

## Scene One: The Agreed-Upon Plan

They discussed the next day's skiing. They would sleep a little later, then together proceed to the ski lift mid-morning. Fine. The following morning arrived, Dad arose early (habit!), drank coffee, and read for two hours. Very pleasant indeed. He then awakened his daughter, and because it was her birthday, served her Cheerios and hot chocolate in bed. What a guy! And, not wanting to be seen as partial to either (a balancing act every parent tries, but ultimately fails at on a regular basis—largely because he has no control over how his efforts are *interpreted* by his respective children), Dad also brought to his son's bed a breakfast treat: ham sandwich, mustard and mayo. So far, so good: the balance was holding.

Now, no normal healthy male of forty-nine years would be so indulging of two other healthy adults. But, remember, he was not *just* a normal healthy male of forty-nine years. He was, in that context and configuration of people, Dad— busting his buns in a rather pleasurable fashion to leave positive memories in the minds of his offspring. He foolishly hoped that these positive snapshots would somehow balance out the numerous pieces of evidence captured in the family album of his blunders, overkills, and lousy timings. This wouldn't happen, but he had to try anyway.

Dad was solidly doing Dad. Son, in his usually hyper-energy, turbo-charged style, sprinted through his breakfast and preparations for the day's attack on the poor, unsuspecting slopes. Daughter, in her usual deliberate and meticulous style, was also planning not only her day's skiing but also the activities surrounding being twenty that day.

None of them was aware of how solidly the ties of their family were bound at this moment.

## Scene Two: The Provocation

Son, now ready to embark, noticed that his sister was not yet ready. In classic five-year-old form, with a whine in his voice, clenched fists, and an almost imperceptible hammering of his right foot, Son turned to his Daddy and pleaded: "What's her problem? She's always holding us up!" Dad, in wonderful style, assured him: "She won't be long."

Unfortunately, Dad was not wonderful. Had he boned up on his Ginott, Gessell and Dobson, he would have made a more "appropriate" comment, like:

"Son, you're really talented in addressing the day with vigor" or "Ready to test yourself on the mountain, hey, Son?" or "You're right; we guys are fortunate to have such a simple morning routine."

Instead, Dad was not only linguistically dull, he was untruthful. "She won't be long" was either an invitation to convince Son that his entire life of waiting for Sister was a total delusion or that Son was destined to become a complete idiot like his father was currently sounding. From Son's viewpoint, Dad was trying to sell a blatant lie, was defending his Sister's slug mentality, and was abandoning a primary mandate of nature: it's the men against the girls.

Dad poured himself a "top off" cup of coffee, confident that his verbal pat-on-the-head had soothed the eager juices in his son, only to hear shouted through the bedroom door:

"Dad says to get your butt in gear or find us on your own!" Masculine alliance was re-established. "Are we here to ski or to have a beauty contest?"

Daughter was cornered. If Brother was in fact the official messenger of Dad's impatient threat, then the messenger must die because of the message. If Brother was acting on his own accord, then he must die because of his disrespect, lack of sensitivity to female complexity, and his basically obnoxious position of Brother. No mouse at verbal battle herself, Daughter redefined Brother's head as a fecal mass and invited him to insert his words into a dark, lower orifice of his own body.

"It's my birthday!" she screamed in four-year-old waves of rage. "Doesn't that mean anything to you!?"

My cup is suspended an inch from my mouth as I await the arrival of the Angel of Mercy to enter my Son's heart and hear him apologize for his sloppy behavior.

"Your birthday means that if Dad had had more self-control, I could have been an only child, and I'd be on the slopes skiing right now!"

I don't exactly remember dropping my cup. I only remember grabbing a wad of paper towels and sopping up coffee and broken pieces of ceramic off the tile floor. I had always suspected Son of being bright and verbally talented. In one crushing blow of his tire tool he had desecrated the significance of Sister's existence and vengefully destroyed the sexual integrity of Father.

Things were not going well between my loving children. So in true parental fashion of intelligence, authority, and responsibility, Dad went for a walk. He knew, "We are in it again."

## Scene Three: Strategy

An old family fight scene had broken out. Six-year-old Son pushed three-year-old Sister, who, in turn, called him a "nu nu," thus driving her brother to retaliation. Daughter ran crying to Papa. Son denied touching her, and Daddy was now called upon to settle it. "Settle it." What a strange and bewildering task that parents are called on to perform. Seems simple (notice that word again) enough. There are several options for "settling it":

a. Listen lovingly to each child's side, then make a judgment call in favor of the most righteous (a strategy certain to offend at least one of the two).

b. Ascertain "who started it," then rule in favor of the victim (a strategy initially pleasing one but later convincing both that the parent stupidly ignores the substance of the fight).

c. Punish both (designed to teach the crazy-making lesson that you are bad just *because* you were in conflict).

d. Hear arguments from both, grant that each has a valid point (then hang yourself from then on to be the sole arbitrator of all fights between your children).

e. Abdicate, refuse to intervene (and in so doing, convince each child on different occasions that there is no reliable parent available for protection or understanding).

f. Upstage the kids' fight by claiming that their conflict has made *you* upset (thus robbing them of the fight being their own and instructing them that every upset is ultimately an offense against Mom or Dad).

You can't win—if, in fact, winning is the preferred illusion of any parent. There is no right way—if being right is what a parent foolishly hopes to either be or model for a child.

So what was Dad to do? None of the options appeal when dealing with grown kids. (Perhaps "grown" and "kids" are contradictory in the context of family.) Nor were the issues quite the same as when Son and Daughter were six and three. Their lives were more complex; their understanding was richer. And each of them had full-blown personal struggles of identity and purposefulness and belonging and future and faith. Each of them had a uniquely designed emotional process, built on beautifully stylized experiences both within and outside the family.

It was the same family structure, with old familiar expectations and predictable, automatic responses. Yet the people were different—older, wiser, more informed, more colorful, more self-sufficient, more self-aware.

To intervene as he might have ten years earlier would have been nothing less than suicide for Dad. To pretend nothing was happening was beyond his ability. It is at moments like this that Dads so clearly realize that God in his evolutionary design intended that children should have two parents: a father to protect them from their mother's solutions and a mother to protect them from their father's solutions. For nothing in creation so incites a Dad to rage as when he thinks he must intervene, knows not how to intervene, and lacks the option to command: "Honey, come take care of your kids!"

So Dad waited. And watched through the peep-holes of his otherwise pleasant exterior, for even at this time in his life he was not beyond feeling compassion and failure at his kids' estrangement from each other. And as he waited, withholding any strategy that came to mind, he began to recall that each child would signal how and when they would seek his involvement—if at all. And if they did signal an invitation, he would then have to decide on "none of the above" as options. Was Dad now bright enough not to try one more time what he knows does not work, never did work, never could work?

More than anything else, he hoped that by waiting long enough, the conflict would fade into oblivion.

Funny thing: it didn't.

## Scene Four: Initial Efforts at Resolution

Over the ensuing two days, Son and Daughter sought out Dad's ear. Son was locked in anger, fearful of losing control and attacking his sister while at the same time unable to let go of the hurt following her abuse. Daughter was locked in hurt and disbelief that she was the object of such abuse from her brother because of her innocent behavior. She sought only his apology. He sought only her death.

Interestingly, neither sought Dad's intervention to make it right. Neither (outwardly) wished for his power to be made present. Neither wanted him to confront the rival child. And Dad remained steadfast in his unwillingness to either confront the confiding child or defend the absent child.

It was here in these several individual talks that the richness of each child's historical and personal issues began to unfold.

Son's struggle was with his own long-standing impatience, his eagerness to go out and get things done, his wanting to be respected by his sister, his battle with his "bad self," his growing faith, his fear of losing face, his parents' disappointing modeling.

Daughter's struggle was with her refusal to be one-down with her brother, her commitment to her positive self-image, her growing ability to focus on single issues, her love for her first playmate and secret respect for him, her recurring need to have someone (Dad) see things her way, her stubbornness.

Indeed, no six and three year olds here. The outside squabble was tiny compared with the intense internal turmoils that were triggered in each. Simple solutions would not apply here. Clever words or attempts at "kiss and make up" would be entirely out of place. But something else, something magical, was taking place. We were talking together about ourselves—substantive talks. We were learning about one another, acknowledging who we were, what we feared, what we wished for. And without planning, without intent, we were forgiving ourselves for being utterly human, utterly imperfect, and utterly loving.


## Scene Five: The Blunder

Dad wanted more. Fool. What is it that drives us men to want to close the deal, to make it right, and to leave no stone out of place once it has been turned for exposure? I suspect it is lack of trust in the on-going exchange. I suspect it is hope based on fear that completion and tidiness will prevent (prevent?!) a recurrence of conflict and disarray. I suspect we would prefer a great-looking automobile to a well-running car.

Dad pushed for more. Was it possible that after two days of caution, paternal conversation, and avoidance of direct conflict, the two combatants could face one another, acknowledge their individual parts, and agree upon at least a truce—if not a reconciliation? Was that asking for too much? So, in the condo's privacy, Dad invited them to finish the fight. They tried, but after initial, controlled exchanges about how it all started, the six and three year olds in the presence of Daddy slipped rapidly into the original lashing and slashing. It was déjà vu in spades. In brief, snapshot fashion, Brother demolished the integrity and bloodline of Sister. Sister ragefully reduced Brother to the final part of the alimentary canal and stormed out. Yes, Dad had asked for too much.

He was a bit ahead of the process. Fights, like families, have a life of their own. For there is that fascinating mechanism called "readiness" that stands stubbornly at the door of each of our hearts. It can be nudged, but never forced before its time.

The day ended sadly enough with Daughter encased in her birthday hurt and Son struggling even more with his demon that threatened destruction.

## Scene Six: The Escape

The note Dad left on his bed read:

"Hey—have walked to cafe for reading & coffee. Check with me there. Dad, WLYB (who loves you both)"

It was a beautiful walk through the snow to the ski area restaurant as Dad reviewed the week's events and their family struggle in particular.

How powerful are the forces within a family's political structure. What depth of emotion can be generated by the smallest of events. How stubbornly we hold onto our feelings, our interpretations, our conclusions, our expectations—even as we can watch ourselves from across the room, so to speak, behave in ways we would not want the world to witness.

And yet, that is the very stuff of what family is all about. It is an arena, a meeting ground between our highest aspirations of love, affection, and mutual support and our most primitive urges of self-protection, self-righteousness, competition, and revenge. Our family is where we feel safe enough to expose our most infantile and selfish nature, where we are most vulnerable to being annihilated by the very ones we most trust with our hearts.

It's not easy being in a family, unless it is a family built on habits of severe avoidance and pretense. Being in a family allows us no real escape from either the community of our family members or from the larger family called our species. For so much of what occurs behind closed doors is the re-enactment of emotions and behaviors more profound than personalities or even the multi-generational history of a particular family group. Family events and interactions are as much a recapitulation and sharpening of the richness of the human species as they are a summary of any particular family's brief yet unique history.

There are no quick fixes for real people in real families, no easy solutions, no formulas that apply to more than one episode. No cookbook on "how to be a happy family" or "solving those parental woes" or "making marriage work" can ever do more than offer interesting, mind-stretching comments of the most general form.

Why? Because the incredibly rich and unique moment that occurs between any two people can be neither planned nor controlled by either: it is an event that has never occurred in the history of the universe, nor can it ever be duplicated. Historical precedents, yes. General patterns of behavior and style and family configurations and recurrent issues—all, yes. But the actual interpersonal experience in the next moment of time: brand new.

We are a species that has for thousands of years worked hard to maintain some control over our impulses to hurt, maim, exclude, or kill one another. Like other species on our fragile planet, we have developed a vast array of behaviors, rules, and rituals to keep emotions in check and directed toward the safety and preservation of our kind.

But the system is far from a perfect one. When Son takes a cheap shot at his sister because her preening activities delay his fun, and she retaliates with a verbal slash at his manliness, the stage is set for a drama that has been repeated millions of times in millions of homes over the last million years: "Now that the snakes are out of the sack, how do we get them back in?!"

How to put a lid on the feelings flying wildly? How to stop a battle that has begun? How to prevent undue hurt or abuse? How to stop short of irreparable damage?

At this split second of a tussle between two members of a family, the question is not the speculative "Now, why did this start?" Nor is the pressing question a philosophical, "How could this have been averted before it erupted?" Something more urgent is at hand: "How do we stop this wagon before we go over the cliff?!"

Outside the family, we have numerous controls that stop, mediate, deflect, and absorb our emotions. Not so easily done between brothers and sisters, parents and children, wives and husbands.

The coffee was warm and friendly at the cafe, as Dad thought and read and jotted down notes on napkins. Looking up, he saw Son standing at the table, eager to hit the slopes with a vengeance. Just checking in. See you later, alligator.

Soon thereafter, Daughter appeared, dragging behind her the ragged edges of her departure scene the previous night. She, too, was ready to ski, but not before seeking Dad's validation of her efforts. He did; she split. Afterwhile, crocodile.

## Scene Seven: Did I Miss Something?

Later that day, Son and Daughter were skiing together, laughing, kidding, and challenging one another. Several "happy family" photos were taken, lunch, togetherness.

After two-and-a-half days of loose snakes, they were again sacked. How? Fatigue? End of venom? Personal issues re-claimed? Time apart? Wish to end on an up-note? Awareness that each was more than a brother or sister? Distractions? Dad's removal from the scene? Dad's availability to help diffuse some of the heat? Prayer? Each seeking out other non-family sympathizers? Gaining some perspective over time?

All of the above? None of the above? While Daughter and Son each moved through their struggle in his and her own historically summarized fashion, they had some things in common—experiences which the human species generally cherishes as a way out of the fog of discord.

Each of them needed to express the range of emotions provoked by the affront of the other.

Each of them needed to know that it was safe enough to allow such expression without fear of reprisal for either the literalness of their expression or for the fact that an expression occurred.

Son needed to know that he was heard by his sister. Daughter had a reciprocal need.

Both needed to, at least initially, blame the other for the discord. (Sorry, folks. In spite of what the field of mental health has promoted, we do, in fact, blame one another as an opening shot in every conflict!)

Eventually, each of the fighting family members needed to know that the opponent acknowledged some part in the problem, without having to resort to measuring who was more at fault than the other.

Each of them needed time and space to cool down during the span of conflict. This allowed for thought and perspective.

Each of them needed to gain, if not from one another, at least from a friend or other family member, some validation for her and his feelings. This did not require that someone agree or take sides, but that someone recognize that there was a basis in Son's or Daughter's reality to warrant the emotional expressions and conclusions drawn: "Based on where I'm coming from, this is how I felt and what I thought was happening. Is that OK?" Of course!

All of this was woven into the fabric of their unique fight. All was done in the service of simply ending the conflict. Only *later* would they be able to discuss the event and do some problem-solving in their relationship.

Somewhere along the way, each of these two family members faced a fork in the road of their individual struggles: to either careen toward even greater separation and pain or to proceed painfully toward re-connecting with someone loved as well as hated. That elusive element— timing—played an almost insidious role in the drama.

It's not easy to have a fight without Papa settling it for them. It's not easy to stay in the struggle long enough for both to win. But they did. And this time, Dad chose to leave well enough alone.

*Afterthought*   So. Was this a vacation or an education?

Why is it that when "the family" comes together, members re-create earlier, even infantile, thoughts, feelings and behaviors that don't fit the current scene?

As Dads, why do our efforts to bring order and tranquillity among our grown children so often meet with disaster?

What conclusions have we drawn about our own fathering as we watch our children struggle?

Why are we Dads so privately hard on ourselves, even when we publicly disavow any serious concerns about how we parented our kids?

# On the Occasion
# of My Son's Fatherhood

*Forethought*   A photo album is a wonderful device. It entices us to
recall our past as a series of happy and loving events.
The human mind is no less creative. We can call up
our past in exactly the way it suits our convenience,
our public image, and our need to see ourselves as
having done our best. We want to remember that we
were good Dads, fair Dads, firm but loving Dads. And
when we slipped on our emotional butts, it was because circumstances forced our hand.

But a bolder writer stands in the wings. For reasons
known only to him and his shrink, he has left us a
profoundly balanced view of his life as a father, taking
the hit for all of his failures, leaving out none of his
love. Rather than bury his mistakes (as all males are
trained to do), he shares them with his son on the
birthday of his first grandson.

In spite of all that I have wanted to
  believe about my efforts,
In spite of my obsession to learn more
  and to understand better,
In spite of my resolutions to be decidedly different
  from them and them and them,

In spite of the help I have received
   and given to others,
In spite of my frustrations and tears
   and renewed attempts,
In spite of my glossy explanations
   about lost opportunity and personal limitations,
In spite of my prayer, my work,
   my seeking for self-honesty and integrity,
In spite of all this, I have repeated in my life
   a failure to modulate my impulsive anger,
   and I have created for my children an abusive atmosphere
   of conflicting love and hate, trust and fear, closeness and
      distance.
I see before me a fourth-generation hot-head,
   a young man swinging between selfless love and abusive
      rage,
   using whatever is available to maintain some control over
      himself.
I weep inside at my failure. I am filled with shame that I
   could not have done more, done better, or at least done it
      differently.
He lived in fear of my anger, and at the same time was
   drawn over and over again to provoke that same anger. I
   lived in fear of his unpredictable and disruptive behavior,
   and at the same time was drawn over and over again to
   focus on those behaviors and to unwittingly reinforce
   their occurrence.
He yearned for my accepting him as he was:
   hyperactive, provocative, non-responsive, non-compliant,
   racing, screaming, disappearing, reappearing. I could not.
   I had not the understanding, the energy, nor the strength
   of character to remain undisturbed by his chemically-
   based behavioral blur. I was reactive, hurtful, remorseful.
   He could only have interpreted my reaction as not loving,
   not accepting him.
For my part, I felt the pain of never being given a chance to
   be accepted by him as his father. He would not let me
   succeed. He tore away at my peace of mind, he robbed

me of what little competence I had. I felt unaccepted by him. When I held back my anger, he pushed harder, demanding of me that I fail through repeating what I desperately tried to avoid. I could not stop him; I could not stop me.

So when I finally despaired, he left—long before he was ready, long before he wanted. I could no longer dance the tragic dance of mutual abuse that the two of us drove ourselves to perform. He left to play out his defiant role to the waiting audience of an abusive world, while periodically touching my life with his, denying me relief, denying me denial.

More than once, I grieved his death. More than once, he entertained being killed, for merely dying would have been too gentle for his driven and self-accusing heart.

Today, he lives: passionately, with great love, with dreams to help others and to simultaneously save them from the sleeping terror that can awaken inside of him at a moment's notice. I admire and love him for his tenacity to live.

The terror and sadness of my own abused and abandoned childhood reaches across time to join compassionately and lovingly with his. Late in my life as a father, I have come to see what I could only have felt as a child, re-lived as a young man, and perpetuated as a confused and frightened young parent.

Some day he will also remember my rocking him to sleep each night to quiet his colicky tummy, singing to him softly.

Some day he will recall riding on my shoulders, playing blocks together, chasing one another, smelling the grass as I mowed around his swings.

Some day he will smile as he reviews the videos in his head of our camping and fishing together, baseball and soccer games, pitching practice on the sidewalk, bicycling to exhaustion, the zoo, reading stories in bed, stoking the fireplace, breakfast at McDonald's, church, Sunday school, donuts, bus trips to grandma's house, piano lessons, drums, Jeanne, Liz, Clyde, the Camaro, the trucks.

Some day he will remember the apartment and chocolate
pancakes and forbidden orange juice. He'll remember our
looking for the house together, our struggle with the
school principal, skiing in Colorado, another bike to
replace the last one stolen, watching *Speed Racer*
together, Spaghettios.

And in remembering these, he will perhaps recall what the
mind fights against: that I loved him in so many ways, that
I was there, that he could count on me. And in
remembering that I loved him, he will then remember
that he was lovable, not just when he was good, but also
when he was not so good.

Now he, my son, is a father. And I wish not to save him or
shield him from his own struggle with a wounded past.
My wish is this: to let him know who I am, who he is, and
that by revealing ourselves to one another, assure him
that I will be there for him and with him in his groping for
competence and joy as a father.

And in spite of this resolve, I know that I will fail if I insist on
making it happen.

Please, God: let me just be there to love him, and let the
rest go.

*Afterthought*   So. Talk about guts!

Which of us would have the courage to acknowledge
to our children how we failed as fathers?

What fears do we have about how we will be remembered, imitated, or blamed should we claim our half
of the family conflicts through which we lived?

What special gift do we offer to our children when we
acknowledge our flaws, our handicaps, our biases,
and our immaturity we displayed in their years of
growing up with us?

How does becoming a grandfather stir us to re-evalu-
ate who we were (and are) as Dads?

# *A Weeny Sandwich*

*Forethought*    Every family has its own unique culture: how things get done, who's in charge, when events occur, what constitutes work, play, togetherness. And each family celebrates its being itself in ways that are recalled by its members as "our way."

Designated holidays and memorial events help us along: they force us to pay attention to values we might otherwise neglect. We are a species that needs reminders.

But does a nationally designated day—like Father's Day—match with my designated Dad? Does our family feel like celebrating the man, and does the man feel flattered by or embarrassed by "the day"?

So wonders the next son: how to fit the day with his family, his Dad with the day.

I've always had difficulty celebrating holidays, birthdays, special days of remembrance. Not that I object to the *idea* of recalling and honoring events or people. What has plagued me throughout my life has been the nagging issue of *how* to celebrate.

So often I have either witnessed or been the victim of how the party was more a fanfare of the party-giver rather than a joyous recognition of the honoree. A cake that a one-year-old is not allowed to touch, a gaggle of eleven year olds in

110

## GREAT FATHER AXIOM
## #261

It is the common father who can accept
and appreciate the acts & gifts of love
he loves;
it the *great* father who can accept,
embrace and cherish the acts & gifts
of love he hates.

starched shirts and evening gowns posed for photographers, gag gifts that embarrass, food that no one can eat, exaggerated lights and artificial music and painfully contrived games—all so often without humor, human contact, or joy.

How many funeral services have mechanically buried our dead?

"Occupant was dearly loved and shall be sorely missed."

"He/she is not dead, only transported."

"We have been blessed by his/her brief sojourn in life."

Many times I have screamed silently: "Excuse me—but are we talking about the same person?! I have a differing opinion! You say that she was a tireless worker, a loving mother, and a devoted wife. All of us sitting here know that in fact she was obsessed with germs, chronically drunk, and terrified of her husband—the guy over there carrying a load of guilt that masquerades as grief."

And cards—how I love and admire the fine art of saying nothing specific about someone in sixty words or less.

"Best of everything on this most important event."

Birthday? Bridal? Burial? Bar Mitzvah? Bon Voyage?

Who knows? Who cares? So long as the record shows that at least a card was received—a token of our hurried lives, our absence, our wish to have really cared. The only thing personal about most cards is the person's name on the envelope—making it entirely possible for the recipient to re-use the card should the sender thoughtfully neglect to sign it.

Flowers are always appropriate. When all else fails, we can splurge on a small or medium bouquet for the person we love or respect or fear or whatever unmentionable emotion can be buried in a bunch of cut roses or carnations. Along with a miniature, low-risk card, again.

Heavens, this is sounding harsh! I don't mean it to be. But what seems to be bleeding through is a sadness I have felt about two issues in our family and in the families of my larger human community. The first is that of celebrating. The second is that of fit.

We say we celebrate marriages of friends, deaths of our relatives, birthdays of our children and parents, anniversaries of our wives and husbands, graduations of sons and daughters, successes of co-workers, the week's end, worship of God. There is always an event (birth) and a person (Uncle Justin), a significant happening (marriage), and its human embodiment (Jean and Joe), a mystery (death), and its visible form (Dad).

But do we celebrate? Or do we attend and watch the celebration from a safe emotional distance? Why have I witnessed over and over again the women celebrating and the men attending? Some exceptions, of course. But look more closely. Carol and Meg and Jennifer and Beth are animated, inquisitive, participating. They sing the songs, they cry unashamedly, they hug warmly, they clap with vigor, they are transported into the event with renewed passion and they are connected with the celebrants with an intimacy that leaps across family boundaries and ethnicities.

And the men? I survey them with puzzlement, wondering if their hidden hearts belie their public attendance. Bodies stiff or shuffling in obvious dis-ease. Eyes stare with emptiness through the person being honored, past the event, escaping even the mystery recalled. They hug mechanically, mouth the standard clichés, stare at blank pages in the song book, smile at passing humor and steel themselves against the slightest hint of out-of-control feeling.

Is there honor in remaining untouched by the profound awareness of birth? Of death? Of marriage? Of the universe of touchable mysteries? Do we men so fear being carried along by life's river of love and loss and pain and joy that we grip tightly a rock buried in its bank, proving to ourselves that we have beaten the river? Is our ultimate competition a contest between us and it—life? What a wonderful microcosm of this idiocy as we stand tight-lipped and tight-assed in the face of a young couple stepping into the dream of marriage or a child dead from AIDS.

Men have trouble celebrating. We'd rather attend. We'd prefer to remain disengaged from the uncontrollable event we are witnessing. We'd prefer to remain detached from the person being celebrated: but for the grace of accident and time, we could be him (or her!). To step into the power of the event and to personally identify with the persons spotlighted would render us embarrassingly human and vulnerable—a specter we prefer to relegate to the privacy of our caves.

Then there is the question of fit: does the celebration fit the person? Does the person fit the celebration? Does a sermon on the virtues of the Church of Christ fit the Baptist corpse being buried by a predominantly Catholic and Jewish congregation? I have attended such. Does getting drunk and destroying public buildings stand as a fitting celebration for winning the football division championship? Many boys think so. Is a man celebrating his unashamed personal relationship with his God when he knows his church membership card self-destructed at age eighteen and he only marginally "assents to" or at least "does not violently object to" the dogmas celebrated? Lots of men secretly know there is no fit.

Does a family stack the gifts, flock the tree, send a spray of roses, make the 9:30 service, mail a card, do the ritual, make a showing, drop off a pie, stuff a turkey, pick up some candy, wire a fruit basket, leave a message, offer a Mass, sign the register, mail a regret, deliver balloons, bring the wine, take up a collection, draw names, draw lines, draw—as *substitutes* for celebrating together, being together, touching, moving, and knowing together?

Does a family bake a chocolate cake and load it with sixty-five candles to be blown out by a Dad suffering from emphysema, allergic to chocolate, and diabetic? Is this a fit? We did this very absurdity without ever thinking about fit! Until this year when some unfettered granddaughter wondered out loud: "Why don't we celebrate Father's Day in a special way—a way that reflects our family culture?"

"We don't have a family culture," objected her brother, "because we hardly ever do something twice. We're a fly-by-the-seat-of-your-pants family."

Father's Day had for years been a basically low-keyed day in our family. In fact, no-keyed would be closer to the truth, since it had been semi-celebrated as an almost after-thought compared to Mother's Day. Perhaps this is as it should be, for no matter how romantically we try to hail our dads, they usually are part of the background to the family novel: *Life With Mother.* Definitely cards, calls, carnations and catering on Mother's Day. But Dads—well, how about one of the above?

Besides, dads don't really celebrate. They rather join in by hanging around some event occurring in someone else's honor. Dads prefer to show up, stand politely with coffee and chat, then become flustered with awkwardness and feigned excitement if attention is directed their way.

So when we decided to do Father's Day, we agreed that the event should be mostly in honor of Grandpa, with my kids sneaking me, Dad, onto stage right. How would we honor Grandpa in a way that he would enjoy and that would personally reflect his lifestyle and our family?

Lunch at the usual cafeteria was immediately shouted down as same old same old. How about cooking Grandpa's favorite low-cal dinner of lasagna, potato salad, lima beans and cornbread? Not this time.

Grandma suggested that we could create a two-hour group nap and snore in unison. Grandpa didn't think that was funny.

Why not stage a family sit-in at the Country Cafe where Grandpa hangs out, drink eleven cups of coffee each and exchange views on last night's TV weather report? Boos and laughs.

"I've got it!" screamed the granddaughter: "We have a family custom. What do we like to do when we come to Port Arthur? Crabbing."

It was brilliant. And it was unanimous.

Father's Day, 5:15 a.m. We arrived at Grandpa and Grandma's house, rousted them up, loaded two vehicles, and blazed out for the bay. A quick McDonald's stop fortified us for the celebration day.

What a time for Grandpa! In sweltering ninety-degree morning heat, he graciously cut lines, tied chicken parts, retrieved nets, carried ice boxes, held dogs, handed out cold drinks, and cheered us on in our endeavor. After four hours of nonstop crab entrapment, we loaded up ourselves and four dozen victims for the trip back.

Steaming crabs and corn filled the old house with historic aromas as we laughed and recalled the day's victories. Then, gathered around the table, we gave thanks and began our Father's Day feast. A pile of crab and shrimp covered the table.

At the head sat Grandpa—a man who (I forgot to mention) hates the sun, would take a bullet before giving up his air-conditioned den, whose idea of the great outdoors is a quick trip to the shopping mall, and whose utter distaste of seafood is a long-established family truth.

But there he sat, proud as a peacock. He was eating without a care his favorite lunch: a weeny sandwich. Happy Father's Day, Dad.

*Afterthought*   So. Does the gift fit the man being honored?

How many times can we recall going through the polite motions of a "celebration" and being left untouched by the event, the people, the meaning?

What prevents us from becoming personally involved in a birthday, a wedding, a funeral, a holiday? What keeps "it" at a distance from "us"?

Why have we struggled with the whole idea of celebrating? What is it about being joyful with or for someone that leaves us cold or at least hesitant?

What do we really share together that would ignite our imagination to honor and preserve its memory?

# Requiem for a Gentle Man

*Forethought*   So what are those qualities that define a man in western cultures like that of America? We look to a type of man that represents the finest of maleness; then we draw up the list of preferred qualities, compare ourselves to the list, and conclude (predictably) that each of us guys is inadequate—as proven by the list. The idiocy of the process deserves the idiocy of the conclusion.

Some male qualities are easy to admire: strength of character, generosity, career success, leadership. We want to be like those guys. But what does a son say about a father who failed so often he died largely unknown, his funeral largely unattended? What about that man's qualities of silence, gentleness, and near-invisibility?

We sit respectfully on our funeral parlor bench and listen as a man describes his father with words we wish we could have said.

Thank you, Reverend Williams, for your words of love and encouragement, grounded in Sacred Scripture.

117

On behalf of myself, my brother and our mother, we wish to thank all of you for being here to honor the death and life of my dad, Kenneth. Following my comments, his grandchildren would also like to share with all of us their thoughts and feelings at this sad time.

Kenneth will not be mentioned in any history books for great deeds, fame, or wealth, for he lived an ordinary life like yours and mine. He grew up an unenthusiastic dairy farmer, failed to complete school, and joined the U.S. Air Force, where he spent the duration of World War II sorting mail in England. He joined his father's construction company and worked there till he led it into failure twelve years later. He subsequently failed at running a machine shop, then failed at running a dredging company, then failed in a ceramics business.

Three successes he did have—all with his wife: a marriage of forty-five years; ,adopting and raising as his own, two sons; and a pet shop enterprise of twenty-nine years.

In the end, he failed to beat the odds of smoking for more than fifty years.

When someone dies, we take the opportunity to review both that person's life and what our connection with him was.

There is a powerful impulse to want to sum up his life in one phrase, or even one word. Like: "He was a nice person, a hard worker, a loving parent, a man of faith."

And while these and other statements might describe something about my Dad's life, my mind searches even more. I wonder what quality of his personality best states who he was at his core. What one thing best describes his life. What one word would sound a familiar note for all of us who knew him in our lives with him.

I think that one word is: Gentle. He was a gentle man. Not weak, not soft, not withdrawn, not shy. Gentle.

Gentleness is not an easy quality to have in a world of men, in a world of business, in a world of uncertainty that we

all share. Gentleness is not highly regarded in the world today.

People are not always sure how to deal with a gentle man.

Some of you saw his gentleness as a chance to take advantage of him, to steal from him, to rob him of his job and his integrity. You thought of him as unworthy of respect because he was so respectful and trusting of you, easy to hurt, slow to anger, almost incapable of revenge. You did not understand gentleness.

Some of you felt nervous and even frightened by his gentle nature, and so ridiculed him, belittled him, and tried to make him feel ashamed of his gentleness. You accused him of not being a real man, when in fact he was more real and more manly than those who knew not how to be gentle like him. You did not understand gentleness.

Still others of you could not see his gentle side, and so blamed him for being quieter than most, accused him of not taking charge, and claimed he had no strength of character. Yet he had a strength that drew people to him. You did not understand gentleness.

So with so much going against him, why did so many people love Ken? For the same quality: his gentleness.

His gentleness allowed him to blend in with whatever family or friends he found himself. He was west Texas and Cajun and Italian. He was Baptist and Catholic and Jehovah's Witness. He was pot roast and potatoes, butter beans and cornbread, lasagna and gumbo, coffee and a cigarette, champagne and popcorn.

His gentleness made you feel that you were the most interesting person in the room. He accepted you as you were, treated you with respect, paid you an honorable salary, invited you into his home, listened to your worries, allowed you to be who you were—not what he thought you should have been. He gave you the recurring gift of letting you be yourself.

He could disagree, without belittling your opinion or your pride. He could agree, without having to win your approval.

He could say, "I don't know," without losing interest in the topic of discussion. He gave you the gift of his willingness to not have to win.

Gentleness is the attitude of mind and heart that allows a man to set aside his own importance for the sake of yours. It is the strength of character that needs to neither compete with nor distract from your sense of well-being. It is his respect for who you need to be, without comment, without criticism.

That is gentleness. That is the kind of man who never needs to be the center of attention but whose absence in death leaves a very noticeable hole in a family and among friends who so took for granted his loving support and presence.

For his gentle love we will remember him.

For his gentle love we will miss him.


*Afterthought*   So. What will we say of our fathers?

For what portion of their lives will we want to remember them; and how will we say that to their families and friends?

Is there a single word that summarizes who our Dads were—a word that defines their unique personalities on earth?

How do our memories of our fathers compare with those of others who knew them?

Can we reconcile the dark side of their persons with the qualities we admired in them? Can we forgive them their humanness?

Can we do the same for ourselves?

# Dispensable Messenger

*Forethought*     Good scientific research is suggestive, never definitive. It points to probable causes, working hypothe-
ses, interesting yet inconclusive findings, and
provocative parallels with other fields of human interest. Molecular structure is curiously like galactic
structure, cellular life is as complex as New York, the
brain is a cavernous chemistry lab, and birds teach
us a great deal about fidelity and survival of families.

Certainly we can only view the world around us from
the perspective of the human mind. This perspective
struggles against endowing other life forms with human biases; while at the same time our scientific
method honors our species as a member of the plant
and animal world, a participant, perhaps even a
leader.

What happens when we learn from studying other
species that we are not quite the noble primate we
like to think **we** are? What happens when embarrassing and damaging information is revealed about the
impairments of men? Lafost, a research scientist,
found out—and it cost him dearly.


It is difficult for me even to begin this document. I am torn
between taking this knowledge with me into death at my
execution tomorrow and sharing this information with a

world unwilling and unready to hear it. In the end it is the same, I guess.

The multiple charges levied against me, my conviction, and my sentencing are rapidly becoming fixed in my mind as some poorly written screenplay produced by the frightened and uninformed for the satisfaction of an audience asleep and disinterested. Nonetheless, I have been asked by a few good friends finally to speak my mind—an opportunity never really allowed me during the "proper" legal proceedings of the past six weeks.

No, I am not some local, much less national, folk hero. Nor am I the only man who has experienced the events I am about to lay forth. And surely, I am not the only man who has suffered the natural and predictable atrocities for having gone through these experiences and openly acknowledged their impact on men and women alike. Simply stated: I got caught, I chose not to defend myself, and I allowed the rather predictable (again) unraveling of our shameful and embarrassing judicial process. I'm not sure why I didn't fight back. I had nothing to prove. Neither did I have any particular wish to die at the whim of the state. Maybe I just wanted to see how far they would go. Or maybe I sensed that I had come to the logical and natural end of my life travel. I don't know.

It must be about 9 or 9:30 p.m. now, since dinner is served at 7:30 here. Not a bad meal, though a bit high on the fat side. A glass of wine, a mint. Good form. I have until six tomorrow morning, and since I won't be sleeping, I will write through the night. Maybe pray. Certainly remember.

Nothing would bore me more than to recount the sequential events of my life, as if I were slowly drowning, not in some body of water but in the juices of my own narcissism. Rather, my memory is a small collection of miniature bridges that connect my experiences as a man with the experiences of men. Certainly my life is unique; equally certain is its similarity to themes lived out by men throughout my and other cultures. The bridges of similarity intrigue me not only because I have all my life watched men hide from their fears and pain but also because I have had the honor of helping many of these same men transcend their loneliness, their rage, their hardness.

My story ended six weeks ago when I was convicted of three crimes against the State, any one of which could have warranted my execution. Silencing me was their only alternative. Swiftness was their desperate position.

Crime #1: "Exposing for public review classified cultural secrets." This punishable-by-death action of mine is also the first event in my life—not from a chronological perspective but in terms of its central place in my history. The year was 1927, when I was immersed in post-doc research at the University of Michigan. Dr. Kris Sharpei and I had been analyzing some data on sexual differentiation in honeybees, and we largely stumbled onto an amazing discovery. We checked and re-checked our study design, we replicated blind surveys using graduate student observations so as to account for our own biased excitement. What we had found was indisputable: the deliberate fertilization by a queen of one ovum with male sperm always produced drones—by negation. That is, the XY or male sex chromosome is essentially a suppressive endeavor; it aborts the natural impulse of the ovum to produce a female worker bee.

As a suppressant agent, XY in effect blocks the formation of femaleness, leaving in its wake a more limited and basically impaired product—a drone. We wondered about the full implications of this negation process and directed our studies to the gender differences that ensued from this process. Our worst fears were confirmed. We found the drones stronger and more agile than their female counterparts, but these qualities contributed little, if anything, to the overall health and welfare of the hive. The one exception was the drones' ability to mate sequentially with the queen (at her initiation!) and to escape her sting.

On the other hand, our study showed the female workers to be more versatile in task skills, more durable in long-term labor, highly talented in communication, more cooperative, much more socially adept, and capable of acting as a non-competitive group to defend the safety and integrity of the hive. They generate their own leadership through on-going consensus, and they spontaneously nurture not only their young but one another as well. For the sake of bisexuality, the drones achieve strength and speed while they carry, buried and unavailable inside their DNA, the finer qualities of femaleness.

Our department chair ordered a non-publication stricture on the work, and the entire staff was threatened with professional death were we to foolishly share our findings with colleagues or the news media. We were, however, allowed to pursue for five years similar investigations into species that included birds, fish, mammals, and especially primates. Everywhere we found the same: the XY male sex chromosome suppressed the ovum's urge to develop as a female, turning most behavioral marker switches to "off," leaving a penis-waving, muscle-flexing, and socially limited male in all but a few of the species we studied. Humans proved not to be an exception to our findings.

From *Apis mellifera* to *Homo sapiens*, we had demonstrated the natural proclivity of femaleness in a developing ovum and the suppression of most of its finest qualities when "attacked" by the XY male sex chromosome.

"Not all knowledge is useful to humanity," stated our department chair, Dr. Kevin Konstable. He was a brilliant man, good researcher, and a fine leader. He was also rather terrified about the possible loss of grant money and probable loss of prestige at U. of M. He was, finally, immovable in his position.

I waited thirteen years before presenting a paper at the National Academy of Behavioral Studies on "The Implications of Gender Suppression in Bisexuality." Two years following, my book by the same title was rejected summarily for publication by The Congressional Review of American Publishers. Thus my first criminal indictment.

\*\*\*

Must be after midnight. I can hear the sounds of reporters gathering down the hall. Shane, the guard outside my cell, is leaving for home. He wishes me good luck as he departs. I wish him good life in his coming adulthood. He looks puzzled and hides his worry that I know what he does not yet sense.

I like Shane. He has been respectful and rather talkative in the days we have shared my imprisonment. He performs his job well, is appropriately controlled, is precise in his manners, and has allowed himself to risk getting to know the traitor he is dutifully watching and keeping. Sadly, he cannot yet get out of uniform when he is home with his wife, two daughters, and elderly father. His bouts of rage have been frightening to his family and a source of shame to himself. He reminds me of San Francisco.

The years were 1966 through '79—Vietnam, the Beatles, the oil crisis. The University of San Francisco was, among other things, a leading center of study in primate behavior. A well-funded grant for research in family violence had allowed me to focus on those aspects of primate behavior that wreaked havoc in zoos and laboratories and established ape communities in rapidly shrinking territories around the globe. My team associates, Dr. Jennifer Tricept and Dr. Doug Gutterig, and I were asking the question: "What are the functional values in primate families of certain male behaviors, including attacking other males, banging on objects, screaming, self-mutilation, forcible sex, destruction of environment?" We wanted to understand why these behaviors occurred, their source, their consequences—primarily because they appeared to be common and frequent but added little if anything to the survival rate of the families. In fact, prior research had already documented that these behaviors disintegrated primate troops, produced recurring conflict, and deteriorated the overall health of the members.

I will not detail here how we delineated the categories and range of "outburst" or "attack" behaviors found in males and almost entirely absent among females. Protective aggression, status assertion, and parental limit-setting were easily documented among females. Such behaviors tended to be clearly targeted, appropriately styled, and terminated immediately.

We saw that males totally lacked these qualities. The male behaviors of aggression contained aspects of violence, unpredictability, and indiscriminate expression. Why? Why is it that males in primate troops, who are so talented in food identification, territorial politics, guarding against threats, exploration of novelties, manipulation of tools, and organization of members, must be also so out of control and violent toward the very troop they lead, protect, and care for—their own families?

Our research findings proved to be quite interesting. We found that when an otherwise highly resourceful and creative male was faced with a situation *he could not control* (a younger male refusing to submit to his status, a female in estrus rejecting his sexual advances, the troop foraging in an area too broad for safety, the presence of a competitive primate troop, a contender for his leadership, or an inescapable cage) he displayed an emotional and physical behavior of attack on the environment around him—mate, infants, community members, strangers, and physical objects. On occasion, this attack behavior was directed not at his surrounding world but rather at himself, resulting in withdrawal, self-biting, starvation, hair-pulling, eating his own feces, etc.

We labeled this behavior "rage." We chose this term because our findings indicated that this behavioral and mental state was not so much an expression of anger as much as it was the expression of *frustration* and *helplessness* on the part of the primate male "demanding" of himself that he be in control of a situation that is not controllable. We came to view rage as the cry of disintegration, the overwhelming scream of desperation, the outburst of a male's inward and outward (simultaneously!) sense of ineptness that is totally unacceptable to him.

All members of a primate troop, male and female, share the recurring need to dispel discomfort that comes from any unmet need or threat. But where we found females *joining with* other females and males for reassurance, safety, and protection, we found males preferring to act alone and either *withdraw* into self-abusive solitary behaviors or attack as individual aggressors, often in the face of insurmountable odds.

In effect we were observing both sides of the same coin: talent. On the one hand, primate males show a high degree of skill and talent in a variety of areas, behaving actively and creatively. On the other hand, when a male finds himself out of talent and unable to manage his environment, he is ill-equipped to back away from the issue, accept his limitation, or even join with another troop member for assistance. His singularity of skill is also his singularity of frustration and explosive abuse, expressed both inwardly and outwardly.

While other research had demonstrated that severe child abuse and/or neglect could severely handicap both male and female primates in their skills as adults, we were able to show that even under the best of parenting experiences, males will, in a sense, cultivate their own world of abuse through their active behaviors of environmental manipulation and recurring frustrations with failure.

As with all primate research, we felt the ever-present impulse to compare non-human primates with humans. We did not. Instead we conducted parallel studies with human families and groupings in a variety of settings, including homes, places of employment, schools, and deliberately formed groups such as AA and prison populations. We published our findings in the *Annals of Social Science*, and, as the expression goes, the rest is history.

Everywhere we found exactly the same results among human males as among our primate cousins: Rage is the behavioral bond among human males who are aggressively *talented* and *self-accusing* in frustration and failure. What human females have in group support, males only marginally experience and use. The proclivity of men to avoid acknowledging incompetence, their refusal to ask for help, their tendency to identify inability as self-failure, their rejection of help when offered, and their simultaneous impulse toward self-punishment and family punishment—all this coincides with and reinforces our most primitive biological heritage.

Subsequent to the publication of these findings, I received formal notification of an indictment for my second crime against the State: "Repudiating the historical and organizational supremacy of men and degrading their status of leadership."

Laughable, of course. But dead serious for the male powers that rule a society while publicly defending the equality of the sexes.

Tonight I am in a state of profound depression and, at the same time, profound humor. A strange combination of emotions. But they are not just emotions. My head aches at trying to contain the contradictions I have experienced in my lifetime: unbelievable technological advancement and the wanton trashing of our environment and human life; explosions of knowledge and the shrinking of wisdom all around me; global cooperation and political sabotage on every continent; expansion of education and a devaluing of learning.

I am dazed by the current political tyranny of men, a final desperate attempt to conceal the truth about themselves, a shameful suppression of data that is already known by half the human race—women. That is the humor. That is the tragic comedy replayed through each generation and finally evolved into today's legislative dogma. The emperor has no clothes. But he and his political, educational, and commercial cronies act as if all is covered and contained.

I laugh and I weep.

\* \* \*

It is now 2:30 a.m. and to describe my third capital crime, I must go back again in time, somewhere between 1915 and 1920. Growing up in a small suburb of Detroit was not easy, yet we didn't really expect it to be other than what it was. Small farms still surrounded the community of Trenton, and, although some travel was still by horse and buggy, the new automobiles were changing our lives forever. Our newly established Trenton High boosted sixty-seven students through the eleventh grade, ours having the largest graduating class of twenty-eight hearty survivors.

All twelve of us guys were on the football team—the fighting Trojans. All twelve of us were also on the track team, the rowing team, and the baseball team. But we were not all athletes. In fact, by the time I was fifteen, I had already noticed that the total number of high school boys broke down into basically three groups: the jocks, the brains, and the blends.

The jocks were all hormones: active, competitive, girl crazy; they stuck together more than they really dated. They were passionate emotionally but guarded in their display of feelings. I knew David liked me because he hit me—hard!— every time he passed me in the hall. They were always shoving one another, breaking things, getting in the way. I envied them and I hated them.

The brains constituted the second grouping. They were the ones that messed up the grade curve in class. They were also an active group, doing special projects, running for class office, excelling in every organization. They competed quietly, scholastically. But I noticed that they were quite individualistic, loners even. Whatever passion they felt, they expressed it not toward girls but toward achievement. I hated them and I envied them.

The third group, the blends, were the people I felt a part of. We worked our buns off to get along, to be accepted, to be included. Social expediency was our driving force, and we competed not to win or to lead but basically to avoid being left out. We had girl friends but not many girlfriends. Our teachers could count on us, as could the jocks, as could the brains. I hated myself while the jocks and brains envied me.

I doubt that any of us guys really saw this group breakdown definitively, but we were all secretly watching one another for cues and clues of adolescent survival. Each of us believed we lacked what was clearly present in the other groups, each of us striving to become competent in the (few) skills we had. What fascinated me about this colorful and profound metamorphosis was not so much which group we were in but how the grouping was part of a serious, almost desperate urgency to carve out a sense of self, a self-definition, with all the emphasis placed on being as "definite" as possible.

We were giving up our flexibility of love for guns, crayons, and books and demanding of ourselves that we limit our focus to either guns or crayons or books. By becoming specialists, we were losing our softness and sense of wonder. By giving up choice, we were hardening inside and narrowing outside. We were becoming only what we excelled at, and we were confusing excellence with personal success. All this I could discern at fifteen, but I could not believe it or explain it until some thirty years later at our class reunion.

At that time I was undertaking sociobiology research at the University of Alaska, examining the pack systems among North American grey wolves. My interest lay primarily in how "in spite of" clear role and status designation in a given pack, a high degree of role overlap and reciprocity contributed to both the survival of the pack as well as maintained a mood of simultaneous respect and congeniality—even playfulness. I wondered about human parallels and I saw our class reunion as a unique opportunity to conduct an exploratory and obviously speculative comparison between wolf packs and human families, adding a longitudinal quality to my data since I had in my memory bank past observations of my high school human subjects.

Because of our small graduating class, four other classes were invited: the two preceding (our high school elders) and the two following (our juniors). As a member of the planning committee, I proposed and had accepted a format that allowed the men and women attending to have separate "gossip" sessions prior to a total evening together. We had an unusually high rate of attendance: eighty-five percent of the total five classes, with men and women graduates almost equally represented.

Our men's conclave took up the entire area of O'Leary's Club, still standing as a favorite sneak-in for local teens, symbolizing male friendship and acceptance today as it did thirty years earlier. For two hours we laughed and hugged and lied, sipping dark beer and soft drinks, nibbling black olives and pretzels. Because I had strategically spread the word about a research questionnaire, the guys generously and good-heartedly took out their pens and cooperated. Several had no pens, some glanced at their table partners' answers, many laughed and read their answers out loud, and others couldn't understand the questions. Some things never change.

What surprised me as well as every other man there was the impact the questionnaire had on them. Gradually, the group's banter became more personal, more intimate, more serious. We humorously agreed that as teenagers we were all anxious about being invisible and being too visible, about sexual behavior and our sexual image, about comparing ourselves with one another's assets and deficits.

It was George Sikorsky who best summarized what happened to us next:

"On graduation day I was scared silly. I had a diploma in one hand, five hundred dollars in the other, and my mom's blessing to use the cash on any college or job search I chose. I knew it was my time to make it on my own. I thought I had to take control of my world around me, swallow whatever feelings I was gonna have in order to plow through, and prove to myself I was a man. I knew I would use whatever skills, knowledge, power, or strength I had at my disposal to make It happen, whatever It was."

We all laughed and cheered in agreement. George continued:

"But I want to confess something to you guys. Even though I kept telling myself that I had to do it alone, that I had to rely solely on myself, I secretly knew I was using other people, depending on teachers, women, friends, and opportunities to achieve my version of success. And I never thanked any of them."

He broke down in tears. Other men wept over their own memories of selfish deceit. From his tears Sikorsky added: "And it cost me my wife, my kids, and my integrity. I am a success, and I am paying the price of pretending I was doing it alone. I am alone."

The room was awash in silent remorse and mutual support. George had struck a common nerve. For some time no one could speak. Tim Connally, our reigning Irishman, asked to share a story with the group. No one objected. He held the table's edge firmly as he spoke. His arms shook.

"I wanta tell you middle-aged meatheads about waking up. My waking up. Before three years ago I was a dedicated, unconscious, dyed-in-the-wool capitalist. And I was dying inside. I worked twelve hours a day, six days a week. I drank every day, hunted and fished every chance I got, took pride in the townhouse for the wife, parochial school for the kids, security. I was living a driven life, chasing the dream I was taught to chase. I thanked my version of God for my blessings.

"Then it happened. I woke up one Sunday to see my wife sipping iced tea and staring at me from across the bedroom. She told me that the previous night I had been admitted to St. Joe's for examination, then released. The car was totaled. The driver in the pickup was in stable condition. I thought she was kidding. She wasn't. I had no recall. She said she wanted two things: that I start AA and that we see a counselor to see if we had anything left to our marriage. I didn't know there was a problem.

"I didn't know there was a problem. I didn't know there was a problem. Can you hear what I'm saying, guys?! I was asleep at the wheel—not just at the wheel of my car, but of my whole damn life! I was being informed by the woman I married fourteen years earlier that I had not ever been present, for Christ sake!

"Outwardly I was outraged at her description of me and us. Inwardly I was dazed and panicky. I had too much respect for her to completely dismiss her statements. And it took me a full year to realize she was dead right. When I honestly looked at my life, I knew I was still trying to be a good boy to my wife, I was trying to prove myself to my boss and friends, I was faking it as a father—hoping the kids would never catch on to how inept I felt as their Dad. I was reacting to the world around me: I was rarely in charge of my own life. At forty-three I was still at Trenton High, performing for everyone. And I had no idea what I personally wanted or how I felt about my life. I prayed I would die without having to ask!"

Several of the men shouted in agreement. Gil Jankiowsky added:

"You got that right, Timmy! It's a helluva day when you realize you don't have control of the space around you, can't have it, and don't want it!"

We all laughed in agreement. Gil continued.

"The truth is, we stay boys, teenagers, a long, long time. Too damn long! But we try to hide it. We keep thinking that we have to escape the control of our wives like we had to escape the control of our mothers, and in the process we never catch on to the one thing we really need to do to finally become adult men—find our own fathers and finally ask them whatthehell happened to *them*! We're doing what they taught us! We're all damn stupid idiot clods!"

We toasted Gil's insight, laughing and moaning at our mutual embarrassment.

"I'd like to say this about that," chimed in Marcus Fox, a twenty-five-year railroad switchman: "Women are not the enemy: *we* are. It was a woman probation officer that gave me my wake up call. I tried to explain to her that the kid had been hard to raise, that the wife and me never agreed on what to do, and that the job kept me away a lot. She looked at me from across her desk and asked: 'Tell me, Mr. Fox: just whose son is it we're talking about? Whose wife? Whose job? As long as its *the* kid, *the* wife, *the* job, you're never going to be in charge of your life. If they are not *your* son, *your* wife, *your* job, maybe you should forget asking what to do about any of it! I suggest you step *into* your life and exercise dominion over yourself and your family!'

"The nerve of that woman! Telling me it's high time I become a man and start taking responsibility for my life before I die! I sent her a bunch of flowers."

It was a magical moment for these middle-aged men. We laughed and cried. We were touching one another's lives and fears and dreams. We were allowing ourselves to claim our manhood in a new and exciting way, borrowing from one another what our fathers had been unable to give to us individually.

The evening's dinner and dance were a resounding success. The women too had spent a wonderful afternoon together. But no one was eager to explain or describe to the other group what had transpired at the opposite sides of town that day.

Six months later I submitted an article for publication in the *General Review of Applied Behavioral Studies* entitled "Family Dominion: Wolf and Human." In it I described the failure of self-reliant control that persists among human males and compared it with the success of claiming dominion and interdependence that is prevalent among wolf males. I detailed how among wolves there is no separation in the Alpha Male between taking charge of his Self, claiming dominion over his pack, and depending on his Alpha Female as a reliable resource to form a life-long partnership.

I noted in the article that this transition from self-reliant control to interdependent management and dominion occurs only later in life among human males—if it ever occurs at all. The article developed into a discussion of the concept of dominion, how grounded it is in the male's awakening to claim his life as his own, how he subsequently claims responsibility *for* and *to* an area of earth, a sector of society, a group of individuals—his family. The concept of dominion was described as an active exercise of interest and care, originating for the first time from the male himself, not from the community around him. Free from duty, he was finally free to husband, in the sense of being a caring overseer of his family and work.

The article ended with a recommendation for further research into the "awakening process" among human males, what sparks the event, how to encourage it, and what societal and cultural issues vitiate against the process ever taking place among males.

Instead of receiving a letter of acceptance or rejection of the article, I received a sheriff's deputy at my door. I had been formally charged with Crime #3: "Openly defaming the national institutions of independent initiative, free competitive enterprise, and the heroic stature of self-sacrifice for one's family." I was not surprised. Hurt, disappointed, angry, but not surprised. I had lived long enough to watch a once-creative culture collapse from the weight of its own paranoia about women, its tragic retreat from small, manageable communities, and its economic obsession under the controlling political party of the land— males.

\* \* \*

Gender suppression, rage, and dominion. These three pieces of work, these three bridges that link men with men, have brought me to this prison cell this last night. While the upside of bisexual reproduction is diversity within the species, the downside, at least for males, is genetic impairment, frustrated self-demand, and prolonged adolescent sleepwalking. Clearer than that I cannot get. Why else are infant deaths three times greater in boys than in girls? How do we explain five times more physical abuse by males than by females, ten times more injuries among boys than girls, eight times more learning disabilities, fifty times more criminal behavior, twenty times more sexual pathology, ten times more suicides, five times more disappearances, and four times more depression (hidden, of course!)?

We males are not inferior. We are, however, impaired, and we compensate quite well. We are incredibly creative and versatile, and we offer the structural genius for people to interact effectively. If we awaken later in life, we can become participants in that social interaction with women that we and they long to have together.

I shall die today, knowing that I have seen and understood these truths. I am not only glad that I chose to announce what I learned but even more glad that I risked experimenting with and discovering my own adulthood before death. I wish for all men that they, too, awaken.

E. Joseph Lafost, *Today*

*Afterthought*   So. Is the messenger killed because of the message? Or because of his bravery?

What biological differences suggest skills that we men have to a finer degree than women? And vice-versa.

What evidence is there that we men take longer to mature than women do? Is this evidence suggestive of biology or cultural training?

If there is an association between rage and frustration, why is it so difficult for us men to make the connection between the two? Or to do anything about it?

How does dominion differ from control? From ownership?

What has retarded our own achievement of emotional adulthood?

# *Am I the Problem?*

*Forethought*   Fathering never quite ends. Even after the kids are grown (translate: largely living away and self-supporting), they are still a part of our lives. It's a time we can play the mental game of "O my God, this is what I raised?!"

Yes, it all comes back to haunt us, or to bless us—depending not so much on how they are living their lives, but rather on the degree to which we can laugh at our clumsy efforts as Dads. No easy task, for fathering is serious business.

Our next writer, Frankie, made a wonderful discovery recently. He learned—again—that while he was racking his brain to identify where he had failed as a father, his offspring was three chapters ahead.

As I turned off the highway and into our neighborhood, thoughts of my workday were already fading into their secret hiding places in my mind, allowing me the luxury of focusing on home, family, flowers, cats, and assorted squirrels that challenge my patience and ingenuity with our bird feeders. It was my evening to cook. Maybe pasta with chicken and a salad. No. My wife had a board of education meeting. Homemade soup for her late return. Soup it would be. I would get some reading done.

Then it caught me by surprise—again: our son's truck, parked at the curb next to the driveway. I tried not to look at it, foolishly hoping for relief in my shaky belief in "out of sight, out of mind." It never worked before for me. Why do I keep thinking it ever will? Some people can divert their eyes, and their minds obediently latch onto the next visual target. I looked away with the speed of a Trappist monk practicing ocular modesty, and the last scene is riveted inside me like a mental tattoo in living color and exquisite detail. Proof of the existence of the devil.

The issue of course was not that the boy's truck was parked at the entrance to our drive: the issue was that the boy's truck was *still* parked at the entrance to our drive. The issue was that he had asked our indulgence to leave his disabled vehicle there until the end of the week, at which time he would repair and reclaim it. Now came the rush of heat up the back of my neck and into my skull—my personal signal of annoyance, which if left unchecked could erupt into rage, which if left unchecked, etc., etc. And with this sudden emotion there was the accompanying thought: "Which week?"

To be honest, I must acknowledge that the question was not exactly a benign request for information. As every father knows, the question was pure sarcasm, designed to express the speaker's frustration and bewilderment and to impress the listener with the urgency of taking action. Spoken in the privacy of one's own cranium, the question is but an inburst that goes nowhere and sours the mood of this day's-end warrior.

"Which week?" has the texture of the great complainer, Job, when he uttered so many times in his life of spiritual dryness: "How long, O Lord?" It is a cry of impatience, of frustration. It is a yearning to know that someone, preferably the responsible party, cares enough to take action. It is the solemn wish that the one who made a promise keep it. And it is a gentle chiding, a loving kick in the rebuttable:

"You call this a week?!"

For it had been more than a week. We were quite solidly into the fourth week of park-and-hide. Our firstborn had yet to raise a wrench to this lifeless vehicle. Neither had he attempted a diagnosis, a referral, or even the mention of its presence at curbside. In his world the truck, now stored, had disappeared from his reality. What he failed to appreciate was that it had not disappeared from mine. In sight, in mind.

I pulled into our driveway, nudged between two cats to the left and shrimp plants to the right, stopped, and turned off the engine. Had I the skill to turn off my mind also, I would be a different man today. I would be able to move on, unencumbered, to the day's next calling, deal with today's little problems without yesterday's contamination, and be a living example to my family that "the issues of the day are sufficient thereof." But what the ignition key can do to my Buick, it cannot do for me: stop me.

My internal engine raced as I sat behind the wheel, staring through the windshield at a wash of hibiscus blossoms. I am hearing myself review potential one-liners that when spoken gently and lovingly could move our son to tears of appreciation and instant truck action:

"Whatthehell is that parked in the street?!"

"Anybody seen a good truck lately?!"

"Whose vehicle is it, anyway?!"

"Waiting for a miracle?!"

"Do I have to get upset with you kids before anything gets done around here?!"

Suddenly my cranial heat wave changed into a cold chill that backed its way down my spinal cord, weakened my shoulders, and dropped my jaw eleven inches. The car motor was dead off, but I'd just crashed into a wall. That last blast rather caught me off guard. A multi-layered déjà vu: *Do* I have to get upset before a child of mine starts, pursues, or ends a task? Is my emotional outburst the missing piece in the recurring drama between me and the kids for jobs unfinished?

I didn't want to think about it. Too scary. Too self-accusing. Too self-incriminating. I wanted to think about cats, dinner, hibiscus—anything except this insidious joke just played upon me by those little Freudian pranksters called "slips." Right in the middle of some of my more famous, fatherly confrontations, I became the confronted, pinned against the wall by the slippery reappearance of that universal wail served up through my own paternal voice:

"Do I have to get upset before you do something about your truck?!"

There it was again, now in a more specific and current form. The implications of this invective became embarrassingly clear.

Scene One: Son agreed with Dad on a favor that was to last one week.

Scene Two: Three weeks passed with no action by Son but with growing, silent irritation by Dad.

Scene Three: Here's where things become profoundly complex. For although the issue was Son's, the only one with a problem about it was Dad.

This was nothing new. Even Socrates in 385 B.C. was bemoaning that the irresponsibility of youth was a sore tooth for parents, not for the youth. And how to shift the pain to where it belongs and where learning can take place has challenged the minds of parents and teachers ever since. It remains universally true that whoever is bothered by an event or issue is the one who has the problem, not necessarily the one who owns the issue. Children, being naturally egocentric and self-serving, must learn, usually from their naturally other-focused and family-serving parents, to notice that their issues, their needs, and their schedules overlap those of others in the household. They must learn from their naturally responsible, sensitive, and happy parents that agreements are sacred, commitments are law, and that eagerness to do one's chores without supervision are the hallmarks of family training for life success.

The bad news is that obviously I have failed either to have learned these values from my own parents or to have taught them to our children. The good news—begging for some consolation—is that every other parent in the history of the planet has failed as well. It's all a very lovely fantasy about what we would like to teach our kids, about what we wish we had done, and more specifically, about what we wish we had been able to do.

Reality is otherwise. The core lesson we train our children on is to do nothing until you have to. Wait for the starting whistle. Proceed at the normal pace. Speak when you're called upon. Color within the lines. Follow directions. Stay in your chair. Come when you're called. Eat what's on your plate. And above all else, don't upset your father.

Somewhere around the age of four or seven or twelve, I wish someone—anyone—had taken me aside and explained life's second stage to me:

"Son, it's time you hear about life's second stage."

"Really? What was the first stage?"

"Son, the first stage is what you've been doing: trying hard to be good by doing what you're told and getting their approval."

"Not always. Sometimes I've been bad."

"True. But being bad was merely your occasional decision not to follow the rules. The rules were still the driving force in your life, the force you were acknowledging even when you said, 'no!'"

"Wow. I never knew that. So what's the second stage: doing what *I* want to do?"

"Well, er, not exactly. That's stage twenty-three. We'll deal with that when you're fifty-six. For now, stage two is contained in the axiom, 'Do it, do it right, and finish it: the task deserves it'."

"How's that different from what I'm already doing? I work hard to get good grades at school and at home."

"Excellent question. The difference is in the focus. A good grade, say an A, is what someone else gives you for your work. A bad grade, say an F, is what someone else gives you for your work. Here, at stage one, the focus is on someone else's approval or disapproval of your work. Neither grade is about your own feeling about your work."

"I don't get it. Why else would I do the work if not to get their approval? Isn't that what counts?"

"You could do the work for the pleasure of getting it done well, for the pride in your own performance, for the joy of treating a task in a way that honors the task. You can actually do work for reasons other than their even noticing."

"You mean, like when I sharpen my pocket knife, honing it slowly, checking and rechecking the edge, and feeling good about how well it cuts—even if I'm the only one that ever uses it?"

"You've got it."

"But I can't do that with everything. There's homework and housework and groupwork and godwork where somebody's always running the show and I have to do it their way. I'm too worried about what they will say."

"Well, you're correct, of course. But we're not talking about everything you do. The second stage is about beginning. It's about starting to notice how work gets done. And more important, it's about making whatever work that is required of you your own. It's about deciding that once you have committed yourself to doing the task, even the most mindless chore, you shift your focus from having to do it and from what they will think or say to making the work your own, done with attention, done to completion."

"You mean, even when I don't want to do the job, once I choose to do it, I can actually do it well, and even with some fun if I just concentrate on the job and not get distracted by why I must do it?"

"I think you've got it!"

"Sounds hard to do."

"Not many men even try stage two. Not many men ever make the work they do their own. Not many men ever live their own lives."

"Well, I'm not so sure I want to grow up now."

"Welcome to the club."

That's the instruction I needed. I could have used a parental directive to expand my childhood view of the world of compliance. I wish that someone had taken the time to explain to me that the expression, "There's more than one way to skin a cat," is not about the technology of taking feline pelts, nor is it even about cats. It's about plowing— plowing a field in such a way that the furrows respect the contour of the land, the angle of the sun; and it's about the pleasure of completing the task before planting. It's about attending to a task that must be done, but focusing primarily on what the task is asking of me, what the task and I have together that brings us both to a point of mutual fulfillment and completion. That's what I wish I had learned way, way back then, in time to have tried it well, in time to have taught it to my own children.

Tap tap tap on the car window: "Honey, you gonna camp out or come in?"

That's what I love about that woman—so disrespectful of my psychotic episodes. Just walks right up and breaks right into whatever yarnball of meditation in which I happen to be entangled. Hugs and kisses prepared me for her announcement that the kids have dropped by for dinner. I steadied myself for the coming confrontation. She knowingly smirked at my full-blown ambivalence of wanting to be loving and welcoming, while at the same time needing to clear the family air.

The kids greeted me with warmth and affection, asked about my day, and joked about perhaps moving back in for a year or two, just to catch up on bills and eat real food on a regular basis. Certainly I knew it was humor. Certainly I winced anyway at even the remotest possibility that such would come to pass. And even as we laughed together, I felt the urgency to bring up The Thing while there was a sufficient number of people gathered to prevent either my losing control or my son's missing the point. I waited for a pause, cleared my throat, and glanced cowardly at my wife.

"Say, er, Son, we need to talk, er, about the truck...."

"Sure, Pop. What about it?"

Not a good opening sign. He was either giving me all the lead I needed to trap myself in a hostile move of impatience (which annoyed me a bit), or he had not the slightest idea why I was bringing the darn subject up (which annoyed me even more). I suddenly recalled that some twelve years ago we had competed in a take-home IQ test and he scored twenty-five points higher than I. Next, I recalled that since he was nine I had not beaten him in a game of chess. I struggled for a controlled response.

"Well, it's been more than three weeks now and I thought—"

"Hey, Dad, if the truck parked out there is upsetting you, I'll have it moved by tomorrow night."

The next five seconds are difficult to explain. Once while fishing with a friend, his lure managed to hook my left ear on the backstroke of his cast. Within seconds he grabbed his wire cutters, pushed the hook forward till the barb was exposed, snipped off the barb, then backed the unencumbered hook out of my ear. The relief from pain amazingly overshadowed the anger of having been hooked in the first place. But the mixture of the three—pain, relief, anger—formed a logjam of emotion that defied any adequate description.

That's what the next five seconds were like. I was relieved that we had gotten through the issue so quickly and that a settlement was volunteered. I experienced that age-old pain that I was targeted as the one with the problem. But the anger was the worst of all. It was anger that was again masking my frustration with how the entire issue was framed by my son: that the work of fixing and removing his truck would be precipitated not by his own sense of responsibility to an agreement, not by his pride in completing a task begun, and evidently not by his need for his truck. Closure of the issue would be triggered by the Old Man's upset! And what really burned my britches was that he had once again moved his Knight in such a way as to "check" the King.

I couldn't escape. Nor could he. We were in the game again. All my rehearsal, all my pondering, all my wishing, and all my efforts not to fall into the same hole with him—all of them failed. Or so I thought. There stood the King, challenged to respond by his brazen and loyal Knight-of-a-son.

King to Knight: "I'm not upset. Actually, the neighborhood security patrol stopped the other day while I was out mowing, and he expressed concern about theft, since the truck hadn't moved for so long."

He knew I was running—from being found out, from an old recurring scene between him and me, from loss of control, from my despair that he would grow old as uninformed as I. Our female audience also knew I was dodging. They respectfully and mercifully examined the kitchen wallpaper, straightened the newspaper on the table, and counted the blue and tan rectangles in the floor pattern. They didn't know I could tell they were thoroughly enjoying the match.

Knight to King: "Hey, I don't want you to get upset with the police coming down on you. Consider it done." Check, again.

I couldn't get him out of my face with the same dead rat—the centrality of Dad's mood! How can this otherwise intelligent young man not see that my mood does not determine the sequence of events in his life? How can he continue to move from a task he wanted to do, agreed to do, and seemed eager to do and do well, to becoming totally immobilized until cued into action by his father's irritation?

King to Knight: "Hold it a minute. What does my being upset—which I am not (lie!)—have to do with your just doing what you agreed to do? How do I and my presumed anger become the key factor in and sole distraction from you doing your own work? Your truck and its care is not about Dad: it's between you and your truck."

I felt strong, steady, even brilliant. The juices were flowing. I was within throwing range of demolishing his defenses and extracting a surrender, if not provoking a growth-producing insight. This time it would be different, I assured myself.

He got himself a glass of water and leaned against the stove, legs crossed, face smiling.

"Dad, you're getting upset, but I'm not going to mention that. You just don't get it, do you?"

"Get what?" I felt the floor tilt slightly beneath me.

"That I do those things you wish for me—out there. But in here, when it's you and me on the board, it's a different world."

"Board? What board?"

Smirking broadly: "The chess board."

All the air in the room suddenly evaporated. I was choking on the reality that he must have been reading my mind or at least my journal. Which I don't keep. He continued his charge.

"Remember when we used to play chess? You were always talking, trying to teach me a lesson. You were out to capture as many of my defensive pieces as possible. I'm not so sure you ever enjoyed the game, or that you really cared that much about winning. What you wanted most was to be right.

"Me, I concentrated on just one thing: take out the King. You see, Dad, the King and where he is, what he does, and especially what he might do is what my game was all about. The King determined my every move, the King and all his defenses, all his plays, all the time he needed to get himself nailed. It worked for me then, it still works today—anytime we're on the board together. Any questions?"

Questions? Did the cockroach I crushed with a rolled newspaper last night have any questions? Did the fly I swatted on the kitchen counter this morning have any

questions? Of course I had no questions. I think his use of
the word "nailed" fairly summarized the moment.

The crowd was motionless, then burst into laughter,
sweeping me up into their loving acceptance of my mental
death at the hand of a clever underling. And I, stunned by
the sudden reversal of parent and child slots, could not help
but laugh with them at me. It was a magical moment.

He had known all along. He had known what I had
wanted him to learn about tasks from me and he knew he
was free to use that knowledge only apart from me. Even
more, he knew what I did not know—that the serious game
we each played as father-to-son and son-to-father always
focused on the two of us, regardless of the work at hand.
Two worlds, two realities, two sets of rules, two goals. No, I
had no questions. Just profound respect.

Someday when I am being interviewed by ABC news for
my opinion of the greatest moments in the twentieth
century, I will likely list several scientific discoveries,
numerous international endings, and six or seven human
rights and environmental happenings. Certainly I will
include in my report the moving and hilarious moment my
world turned over, the day I tried to hand off the baton of
wisdom to my son, and embarrassingly found out that he
already had it.

*Afterthought*  So. Is it possible that our children are always ahead
of us?

Is parenting really about teaching and guiding; or is
it more like following, listening, watching, and re-
sponding in ways that validate what our children
already know?

Why is being with our children so much harder than
solving their problems?

Can we forgive ourselves for our failures as Dads, and
in so doing give to our children also the gift of freedom from having to get it right?

# Blue Plate Special

*Forethought*   Dining out is not a modern invention. Animals do it all the time. Humankind, at least since we took to traveling from one city to another, has enjoyed the convenience of inns: sleeping in and dining in. What's recent is the separation of the dining from the sleeping inn, a commercial specialty known as the restaurant, and its brainchild, the menu.

Before diners, we ate the only food served by the innkeeper. Now we have choices, lists of choices, pages of choices. We choose not just the food, but also the type of service, atmosphere, price range, and convenience of the place.

The restaurant is a microcosm of a man's life. There he observes time, processes, social interaction, ranking, power, and above all, the slippery issue of choice. Food is important, but it's not primary here. What is primary is his personal experience of his importance on the planet.

Bailey party of four table ready follow me please."

What a surprise: we were told we had a ten-minute wait (my maximum allowed for restaurants) and we were hurried in at eight minutes flat. My lie to the hostess earlier—that we had a plane to catch—probably didn't work this time either. It always puzzles me when things go better than I

had planned. A trick of fate perhaps, setting me up to expect another good occurrence, only to be dashed on the rocks of disappointment again. Not me! I'll keep my skepticism, thank you.

Like four ducklings in single file we quick-stepped behind our under-aged mama duck through the maze of crowded tables, dashing waiters, and dining spectators who glared at us as if we were trespassing on their private feeding grounds. "It's not polite to watch people eat," shouted an inner voice. I wanted to argue that such an instruction was not fair, when *they* were doing the watching as *we* passed through for inspection. I felt the impulse to nod, smile, and wave to my subjects as they poised, forks-in-hand, to bid us a reluctant welcome.

"Will this be OK," mama duck insisted. It was not a question. Not exactly. It sounded more like: "Kids, this is it: take it or wait another half hour." She had led us to a dark corner at the rear of the restaurant, a spot designated for lonely souls, recluses, and muggers. I was right: two happy happenings in a row at a restaurant is too much to hope for.

The four of us glanced at one another and silently agreed to accept the offer. It was the only table available. It was clearly not a time to get picky about choices. The cost of declining was too high for any of us. Carpe Table!

How rapidly our lives move. Eleven minutes ago we were visitors to this dining hall. We had parked in the slot marked "guest" at the door, we had been greeted by the manager, a man who symbolized authority on behalf of the absent owner. And we all knew without thinking about it, that later in the evening with appetites satisfied, we would vacate the premises for our trip home.

But in this magic moment of settling into our chairs and spreading white altar cloths upon our four hungry laps, we had laid claim to this place and this table with a vengeance equal to Cortez driving his sword into the beachfront of the Western hemisphere and declaring: "As God is my witness, I claim this real estate for Spain!" We were now the owners, the squatters, the proprietors, prepared to pay the price of our lease and claiming all rights to demand services that accrue to our dominion. Heaven help those who think otherwise.

We had arrived. My three comrades were busily chatting about the ambiance, good rumors about the place, hunger, the pleasure of being together. Even as I joined in the opening conversations and shared with them our friendship, a simultaneous murmuring was overlapping inside. I yearn so much to be able to have only one conversation at a time, one agenda to attend to, one focus, one level, one of anything. Yet it is there: a drama going on inside, competing for attention with the events outside.

"Here we are!" it bellowed between my ears. "Hello. Waiter! Does anyone know we've landed? It's been a whole minute now. Are we out of sight in this blackness? Are you taking a coffee break in the kitchen? Are you arguing about who's table it is? Is this an unassigned spot? Have we come at a bad time?"

The whole matter always seems so logical to me. An arrival is met with a greeting. A presence is acknowledged by being noticed. One event provokes the next event, and the chain goes on. Our natural impulse is to notice and immerse ourselves into events as they occur, to experience what is happening and to be enriched thereby. Dining out together is one such event. The difficulty with also being aware of the chain that links events and their composite parts is that other elements flood our minds: sequencing, timing, pacing, cause, effect, duration, intensity, beginning, finishing. The very process itself has a life of its own, a color, a weight, and a dogged tenacity to compete for importance. And for those of us so cursed with this double vision, the choreography becomes as captivating as the dance.

The restaurant business stands or falls on three basic premises: taste, texture and presentation. The first two, while not easy, are achievable on the stove. The third, presentation, encompasses the entire range of the event of public eating from the moment we enter to the moment we leave. Presentation is the stuff that competitive restauranteuring is made of, that wonderful interfacing between pan and palate that brought us here, and not someplace else.

What seems so logical to me is not so obviously agreed upon by the rest of the world. And though my anxious tummy is humming, "All the world loves a prompt waitress," the world we are currently visiting is singing: "Take a number and wait in line."

"Good evening," he belched. "I'm Chuck and I'll be your waiter tonight. Can I get you something to drink?" We were rolling again. I was glad. I noted to myself how easy I am to please when things go correctly. (Translate "correctly" as the way I have preplanned them, my way). The secret, though, was: what was Chuck's way? I surmised that he had his own agenda, his tried-and-true delivery, his established sequence of events, his little boxes in his brain marked, "First you, then…, and then you…." How to tap into that scheme was the first major challenge of the night. For failure to read his mind would result in punishments meted out in the form of wrong orders, delays, and non-appearance.

He's asked about drinks, so we had best order drinks. Should we not want drinks he would trip over mild confusion and be left wondering about our true intentions. The leather wine list was passed around like a dead mouse, largely because our entire group was expert at Boone's Farm and Mogan David—neither of which appeared on the roster. Chuck was gallant: tea for four produced not a flinch. Away he flew like the down of a thistle and returned in less than a heartbeat with our liquid order. He towered over us, daring us to either dilly or dally.

Of all the challenges of dining out, the second remains forever my favorite: not, what food do we order, but were we *ready* to order? It was the moment of panic. Before us we held menus containing forty-six choices, not counting desserts or drinks. Already we had been whisked through

the four specialties of the day, and there stood Chuck with
pen and pad ready to seal our fates. His agenda was to take
orders, ours to discern what we wanted.

"Could we have a couple of minutes to decide?" Melissa
begged in a child-like voice. She had no way of knowing the
damage she had just done. She had asked permission to
sabotage Chuck's momentum. Three people sighed with
relief. One of us cringed in dismay, for as Chuckie
disappeared in the mob of movement, I feared he would
never be seen again. We had defied the god of procedures.
For in stepping off the whirling carousel, I knew that it
would require divine intervention to get back on again.

Waiters are like that. They don't intend to punish the
uncooperative menu readers, dawdling sippers, or endless
talkers at their stations. They just forget the ingrates are
there. At Waiter College they learned the fine art of how to
never make eye contact with a customer until they're ready
to serve him, how to move in circles at a distance, how to
disappear completely. Where, for heaven's sake, do waiters
learn to go? Is there a test limit for table contacts? Will they
self-destruct or flunk the course if they get too close to
customers? Is deafness a prerequisite for graduation?

We were now adrift, time to read, time to compare, time
to go out for dinner and return before our Chuckster
materialized out of thin smoke.

Forty-six choices on the menu: the third challenge.
Anxiety began to settle about the circle like a thick gray fog.
Somber tones and wrinkled brows cast a serious note on our
dark corner of togetherness. The silent matching of mind,
tummy, and wallet was off and running.

"What have we here?"
"Look at that yummy description."
"I can't believe these prices."
"Nothing looks good."
"Who's gonna set the pace?"
"I wish I had skipped lunch.
"Healthy, but I hate it."

"Are we splitting the tab?"

"What will they think if I order this?"

Our meditation was shattered by Chuckvoice:

"So! What's it gonna be folks? What can I get you that you really want?"

What a shot! The most terrifying question in our lives, "What do you want?" is fired like a veiled insult by Chuckshooter. The four of us grip and grit at the challenging question. What did we want? What should we want? What did someone else want? What was the best choice? What was good for us? What is left after a process of elimination? What did I get last time? What can I handle in my condition? Will they change it up a bit? Will I be happy with this? Can I send it back if I don't like it? Does it matter?

What I want is always easier if I don't have a choice. What I get I can live with, when it isn't left to me to decide. There is such freedom in choosing only one sun to watch set, only one body to tend, only one sweetheart to love, only one enemy to hate, only one day to live. How often I have reflected on the Eastern proverb that a man with two clocks does not know what time is! How wonderful to enter a diner to read the chalkboard menu: "Soup, stew or BLT's." And what a tragic commentary on our culture that it takes longer to review the Thataburger menu than it does to be served.

But choose we must, in ways that largely do not match with what we admit on research questionnaires:

"After reading six consumer journals and test-driving eleven comparable models and comparing comfort, fuel economy, and handling ease, I selected the midrange sedan," translates privately to: "Flashy color, great acceleration, and my brother-in-law works at the dealership."

"We chose Wiregate Academy for our daughter because of its scholastic record, cultural richness, and caring faculty" is egobabble for: "Not another school would accept our delinquent."

I'll have the sautéed chopped sirloin with pomme de frit," is really: "I doubt they can seriously mess up my hamburger steak with fries!"

Most of the time we don't know what we want or prefer. Much of the time we are terrified of exposing what we want for fear of upsetting the table, everyone laughing, or being told we certainly could not possibly in our wildest imagination want *that!* We expect to not get what we want, or not the way we want it, or even when we want it. And if we get what we want, we know secretly that we will have to pay dearly for it, or even be punished for having gotten it.

"OK. You got what you wanted. Now live it! And don't ask for anything else for the next twelve years! And don't come crying back to me if you're not happy with it!"

It's as if we are cursed if we ever get what we really want. Life is too hard, too complicated, too dangerous to let anyone know the secret desires of our hearts; so we keep our wishes secret until they become unknown even to ourselves.

"One chopped sirloin!" echoed Chuckbright. "How do you want that done?"

The fourth challenge: can the cook read my mind? Can the cook read? Can he read Chuckscript? Or is the only thing visible on the tab a generic "#27," so that the only data recorded or needed is for the hidden computer? For even as the words "medium rare" escape my lips, I see them disintegrating in the infinite space between me and Chuckdom. Why was I even asked? A #27 is a #27 everywhere in the universe, the product of our limitless ability to standardize, simplify, digitalize, and ultimately to nullify even our tastebuds—our most primitive toehold on knowing what we like. The very proliferation of eating establishments is a living monument to a chef's ability to reduce his entire menu to a single ambiance of flavor: if you crave another, go down the street!

With the exception of fast food drive-throughs, salad bars are the greatest invention in dining in the latter part of the twentieth century. For the salad bar represents a rite of passage into adulthood of eating. Having been granted permission to leave our table, we gathered to graze and compose our gorge before our meal. Some of this and some of that, as much as each of us wanted, return trips permitted. Such freedom.

Who would have guessed that so many food items could be considered "salad." From vegetables to fruit, from fish to fowl, from pasta to pastry. Some of them could have been entrees, some hors d'oeuvres, some desserts (where I come from). But here, at this lighted glass island they are salad because of one common characteristic: here, they are cold. Heat might have catapulted them from this arena to a #18 on the menu—at three times the price. Such a premium we are willing to pay for warming our salads.

Of course our entrees were probably delicious. We were too full to know better by the time they arrived. Of course we commented on the excellence of our choices. Who but an unsquelched four year old would admit, "I hated what I got?" Of course we paid the full price of the tab: no one was willing to negotiate a settlement between expectations and realizations. And yes, of course we left an adequate Chucktip: our image, not necessarily his skill, is what's at stake.

Back on the road we reviewed our meal. Our driver mused, "Whatever became of the Blue Plate Special?"

*Afterthought*   So. Ever wonder why we have such powerful feelings about where we eat out?

What events in a restaurant touch on our personal sensitivities?

What represents a satisfying restaurant experience for us?

How does the presence of family or friends alter our restaurant experiences?

Where in our lives do we have difficulty stating what we want?

Why do we hesitate divulging what we prefer?

Is what we want negotiable?

# The Men's Room

*Forethought*  In a perfect world (an oxymoron, if ever there was one!), humans would learn things correctly the first time, use that knowledge efficiently, and never have to re-learn what was learned earlier. A laughable concept. Nevertheless, we harbor this dream in the deep bowels of our souls, ready to scream at the drop of an uninvited instruction, "I already know that!"

But do we? Does what we once learned fit the current situation? Updating skills to respond to the events of today—contextual thinking—is no easy task. We resist the rules changing in a game, we resent complying with Roman protocol when traveling in Italy, we assume that how we treated one another at home should set the pace for community interaction.

More than anything else, we have difficulty thinking in terms of the social dimensions of our most personal habits: how my bodily functions touch the lives of people with whom I live and work. Sometimes it's helpful, enlightening, and even fun to upgrade what we believe is nobody else's business but our own.

Hello, Sir, and welcome to this audio tour of the Men's Room. The few extra minutes you spend here today may save you time and money in the coming years. Don't be alarmed: this is no sales pitch for a product line; you will not

be surprised by a hidden camera from a popular television show. This is simply a service provided by the President's Office of Popular Services.

You probably noticed that the sign on the door read, "Men." Not "Boys." "Men." This is an unconscious cue that there is no one here who will splash you, push you, haze you, or ask you your penis size. Ms. Peekabit from the third grade room will not make a surprise raid to catch anyone smoking. Nor will the fire drill start while you are just starting a serious production. So relax, and attend to your business.

In a similar vein, you did not see the word "Rest Room" on the door. Only at home can you consider such a room a place of rest, and that only by family agreement. A committee of our Production Efficiency Experts has done sufficient research to demonstrate that this could better be termed the "Focus Room"—a room in which to spend time set aside in your busy day to focus on the efficient and thorough resolution of physical necessities: bladder, bowel, cleansing and grooming. By attending consciously and directly to the specific functions you will be performing, not only will you enhance your skills in muscle control and clothes manipulation, but you will experience a high degree of satisfaction that is unparalleled in your other daily endeavors. Concentration, not speed, strength, or pressure, is the key word here. Your cooperation *with* your body, rather than forcing or demanding or fighting *against* your body, will usually produce outcomes with ease and pleasure. Now, let us proceed.

The white porcelain receptacle to your left is marked number one. It is usually referred to as a "urinal," although it has been called "bucket," "trough," "drain," and "jaw" (occasionally resembling the gaping bite of an adolescent hippopotamus). It is called a "urinal" for a particular reason: urinating. Surprisingly, it is not a garbage can, an ashtray, nor even a toilet. You will notice that it is designed to minimize splash, conserve water, save time, and maximize access to toilets for more substantial activities.

We have for your convenience posted above the urinal a list of helpful procedural suggestions. I shall recite them to you as you read along, thus allowing you to use both visual and auditory skills to focus better on this exercise:

1. Stand close enough in order to urinate downward. Distance contests are a part of your past, while accuracy is a compliment to your pants.

2. Use at least one hand for appendage control. Freestyle may look great but it is a distraction.

3. Aim for a depression or curve in the urinal wall. Splashguards and screens are, unfortunately, often trash-laden.

4. Urinate *into* the urinal, not on its edge, not on the wall, and not on the floor. Wet floors are dangerous and smell bad.

5. Look forward or downward only, never to the left or right, even if you are speaking to an acquaintance. Side glancing is obtrusive to others.

6. Remain in close proximity with the urinal until emission is terminated and appendage is retrieved.

7. *Flush*, please. No one, not even you, likes a marked and smelly urinal. Please, *Flush*.

8. *Wash* your hands, please. More on washing later.

Excellent. You will notice that by following these simple suggestions, your *focus* is sharp, your concentration keen, and your task is accomplished with a relaxed, though deliberate, pace. Now we shall proceed to number two, the toilet.

The doors you see to your right are entrances to the stalls—an unfortunate term that conjures up images of barns and animals, horses especially. A better and almost lost term would be "privy," the historical outhouse that had a clear and definite human purpose: private bowel movements. When Sir John Herington improved the flushing system and brought the whole affair indoors, the logical place for its use was the toilette—the grooming room of the house. The part of the system on which you are about to sit then took on the title of "toilet."

Before stepping inside, Sir, you will notice that the stall doors have an opening near the floor. This is to alert you, by a mere quick glance, to the presence of shoes and rumpled clothing indicating the likelihood of an occupant and user of that stall. Should there be some doubt, it is proper to knock at the door for assurance of the stall being vacant or taken. Unfortunately, should *you* be using the stall when someone else knocks, there is no agreed-upon response to the knocker. Some suggestions are "Yo!" "Yes?" and "Not here." Now, take a look and, if empty, please step inside.

Very good. Latch the door securely. This is to ensure your protection from those who fail to look or knock. Before you is one of the finest examples of simple design and efficiency. Like the safety pin, the modern toilet, also known as a commode, almost defies improvement. Notice first the seat. It is round or oval shaped, often having an opening at the front. This seat opening is convenient for easier urination, observation, and disposal of various items during the toilet's use. The dispenser to your left contains sanitary seat covers. Remove one now and arrange it so that the middle part hangs leisurely into the bowl water, while the outer part rings the toilet seat. In the event these "toilettes" are not available, you can easily construct one quickly with toilet paper—if you so desire. Please turn, lower your trousers and shorts, and sit comfortably facing the stall door. Thank you.

There now. We have for your convenience posted on the door a second list of procedural suggestions. We all know that toilet training began somewhere between two and three years of age. And without the slightest criticism of your earlier trainers, we would like to offer an update on your B.M. style. As before, I shall recite the list of suggestions as you read along, allowing you once again the greatest opportunity to retain and recall for future use these helpful hints.

1. Focus: Your single objective is to achieve a bowel movement, comfortably, without pressure, voluntarily.

2. Focus: You are not here to produce *the* great B.M. of all time, nor to save it, nor to admire it. A bowel movement will do fine.

3. Focus: You currently own this stall. Sister Mary Maraudus will not be banging on doors to smoke out boys who love their peepees or escapees from algebra class. This is your place now.

4. Focus: Concentrate on the rhythm of your body pushing, then relaxing; then pushing, then relaxing. Back and forth, down and up, out and in. It is nature's way. No forcing, no teeth-grinding, no bracing between the stall walls, no pressure.

5. Focus: With movement comes a sense of victorious relaxation, an impulse to look, and a moment of waiting for a renewed signal of further activity.

6. Flush! Do not wait for more to happen. Do not wipe yet. Flush! Please. And in so doing, you eliminate the collective odor that has repelled mankind for 150 years. It's as simple as that.

Saving, admiring, and savoring of your "Ah yes, that's me" aroma is not in keeping with the public domain of restrooms. Do all that at home if you wish.

7. *Now* wipe. Your body is your friend. He will care for you, hold you up, allow you successful and pleasurable living *if* he is cleaned regularly and properly. Use a generous amount of paper from the roll to your right. Your hands are about to re-cloth your body, and your clothes deserve unsoiled hands. Good.

8. Stand, dress, turn, and flush again. Please leave the stall and proceed to the wash and grooming area. Thank you.

Stop! I am sorry, Sir, to address you so abruptly, but your impulse is to go directly from the toilet stall or urinal to the door. This is the most critical moment in the Men's Room. For you, like the forty-eight men ahead of you today and the seventy-six men behind you, have not yet thought through this moment.

Please Focus. Look at your hands. Now glance at that door handle. Now back to your hands. You have just urinated, fondled your genitals, splashed urine, had a bowel movement, wiped your bottom, and unlatched the stall door. You are about to reach for a door handle that has been grabbed by hundreds of men ahead of you who have also urinated, fondled, and wiped, and they too impulsively, even rebelliously, skipped washing their hands. And *no one*, not even the maintenance staff of this building, *ever* washes that door handle.

Think about it: you were about to mix it up with three hundred crotches and rear ends, adding your own to the collection! Leaving the Men's Room unwashed means that you will use those same unwashed and community-marked hands to eat your lunch, wipe your mouth, scratch your nose, welcome your clients, hold your children, and make love with your wife.

Focus on your hands. They are your most important bridge between you and the people of your world. More illness-causing material is right now on your hands than you will find anywhere else on your body, and you are about to risk, by reaching for that door handle, increasing your contamination potential a hundred fold. Your hands carry health and affection; they also carry the seeds of illness. And you have a moral responsibility to your family, friends, and acquaintances to treat them with respect, including respect for their bodies. Think about it.

I speculated you would agree to approach the wash basin, as you are now doing. Thank you, Sir, for your sensitivity and caring. The few seconds you spend before this sink will change your life.

Help yourself to a small amount of soap from the dispenser before you, for washing without soap is equivalent to not washing. Wet does not mean clean. Soaped and rinsed means clean. At eleven years of age you were in a rush, so that the steps in a handwashing moment felt like gigantic roadblocks imposed on you by your mother to rob you of your real life. Soap came to represent Mom; as you grew in your cleverness to avoid her, so also did you avoid her symbols—like soap, like washing your hands.

Please, Sir, look into the mirror before you. The man you see reflected therein is not eleven. You are older and, yes, smarter now. This is your body you now are caring for, regardless of your past. And in caring for your body through regular cleansing as you are doing, you are showing love for people who are important to you. Your President wants to encourage you to Focus on your health and not to violate the integrity of your body. You can have both if you choose.

Help yourself to a couple of paper towels. Again, you are not in school and thus limited to one of this and one of that. You deserve dry hands, regardless of what it takes. Very good, Sir.

Now take a shot. Rifle it, lob it, dunk it, drill it, underarm, hook, sidearm, curve. Whatever tickles your fancy. We request that you keep two distinctions in mind. The first is that the floor is not the waste paper dump. The second is that your responsibility for your paper shot ends the instant your wad enters the dump, not on the floor, not the sink, not the toilet. And should, on occasion, the dump be full, please use your towel to compact the load a bit. Thank you.

While you are combing your hair and adjusting your clothes for departure, you are probably thinking again about that door handle. Now you are Focusing! That handle is a problem because even though you have taken responsibility for your hands, perhaps others have not. By reaching for it, you cancel out the good hygiene you have just accomplished.

So the President's Office is making the following suggestion: for this entire year, while these Men's Room procedures are being implemented throughout the country, we recommend that you use an additional paper towel, or the one with which you have just dried your hands, to place between your hand and the door handle. One or two practices will demonstrate how easily this is done. And the towel? Now you know why there is a trash can just outside the Men's Room.

On behalf of your President, I wish to thank you for your patience, your cooperation, and your willingness to focus. More than this, the men and women in your life thank you!

Have a good day.

*Afterthought*  So, can old dogs relearn old tricks, and better than before?

Why do we resist following instructions, even those that are clearly for our benefit?

In what ways do we have a responsibility to other people regarding our personal habits?

Does the privacy of our homes delete our respect for others, our sensitivity for their feelings, and our need to model adult behavior?

To what degree are we still skipping steps, behaving immaturely, and taking advantage of others—just because we are not caught at it?

# *I Am Not Myself Today*

*Forethought*   Nothing stretches our imagination like the giant category we call "life." Nothing focuses our imagination quite like one of life's subcategories: death. Men put a lot of energy into dealing with death.

We depersonalize "it" from "us," personify it as the Grim Reaper, run from it as though it were the enemy, plunge into it as though it were the great validator or vindicator, hide from it as if it were one's dogged pursuer, fear it as if it were man's worst negator, promote it as if it were a service, eulogize it as if it were the answer.

We would prefer to do anything except allow death to be an integral part of our personal experience of living. We want to manage death, rather than allow our death to manage how we live our lives.

Our last writer thought upon his death, not each evening as he lay himself down to sleep, but each morning as he struggled to his feet, and asked:

"How will I wish I had lived this day?" His eulogy of his life was read for him at his memorial service.

You're all probably wondering why I asked you here today. (Sorry, I've spent my whole life wanting to use that line, and the occasion never occasioned.)

Thank you for coming. Actually, this event is really not my first choice. I mean, this.business of a formal acknowledgment of my death. I would have preferred, just for the fun of it, to have executed my Plan A. Plan A was that upon learning of my impending demise, I would hop a plane to Canada, bus myself to a remote northern village, backpack three days into life-infested wilderness, and spend my remaining days absorbing the beauty of early-winter's snow and the gradual numbing of my senses. My remains would be consumed by foraging wolves and diligent ants.

For dramatic effect, I would thus have mysteriously disappeared. And because no trace of my physical self could be found, my actual death would remain a doubt— indefinitely. Sightings of me would proliferate. Theories of plots and conspiracies would appear in the news. The kids would grumble (privately, of course) that my estate has been sequestered pending further investigation. And sales of my books would skyrocket in the heat of speculation about their author. What fun!

Then, when a memorial is held in my honor, the presiding speaker would say:

"He is not here. He is…is…where the hell is he anyway?!"

Then the great cycle of my brief existence would be complete, starting from my very first words at birth: "Where the hell am I anyway?!" I would have arrived and left with basically the same question being asked.

That was Plan A. But as we all know, we usually don't get to do Plan A, those being our dreams, our wishes, our plans, our obsessions—all of which we must renegotiate while we are largely limited to Plans B, C, and D.

This event is Plan B, hopefully designed and executed by those who loved me enough to perpetuate just a bit longer my love for humor. You have this opportunity to be excused from work and family duty to enjoy some good food and good fun. And I, in a way that is immensely dear to me, am able to be with you without being here.

Like each of you, I too have wondered about the naturalness and the unknowable event of death. And if I have learned anything about life, it is this: that nothing ever ends totally. Nothing is ever finally over. Not because of faith, or wishing, or fear. But ontologically. It is the stuff of life that life lives, even beyond our arrogant mental capacity to segment life into events. Life always is. Life never begins at some clearly definable point in time. Life always is. Time, beginning, ending—these are all useful but hopelessly clumsy ways we mark and measure our own experience *of* life and our participation *in* life.

Obviously I could not know quite how my participation in life would change as a result of my death, but here is what I have surmised.

First, it is you who have experienced my ending of this life, not I. My experience is something else.

Second, you have lost me, but I have taken you with me. You see, when I die, time ends for me. More precisely, when I die, time collapses. And in the instant of my life transition from this life experience to the next, all time—all time—transpires. Meaning, of course, that everyone who lives after my death, you, your children, all people till the end of time, have also lived your and their entire lives, have also died, and are there—here—with me.

You have said good-bye to me; I am saying hello to each of you here in my (and your) timeless experience of life that we have, all together, at the same timeless moment, as we each step through the window of time we call death. We each leave time-filled life separately; we arrive here the same instant together. We say good-bye to each other in dying; we say hello to all of us together through death.

Clever? I thought you'd like that. Theologically correct? It doesn't matter, since all theology is humankind's guess at God's unfathomable presence. Humorous? Of course! Why else would the best mystery be saved for last?!

But keep my speculation on death a secret: the world is not ready for so simple a view. Ponder on your own the possibility of something so beautiful, so surprisingly Christic. And smile as you imagine that dramatic moment of timeless transition, when we all experience together that burst of awareness—in laughter.

I want to confess something now. I want to confess my struggle with…love. Even writing the word makes me nervous, probably because since my earliest recall, "love" had been so avoided in the language of my family and so bastardized by the culture in which I have lived. For the first twenty-five years of my life, I never realized something: much of what went on around me was love. I was told my parents loved me, but I had difficulty believing it. I believed God loved me, but I had difficulty hearing it. I knew my dog loved me, and I loved my dog. It was all in my head; my heart never felt it.

It was my children who opened my heart to the warmth and joy and pain and longing of love. But even then, I doubted my ability to love without counting the cost, to love without having to be appreciated, and to be loved without having to either deserve it or later repay it. I struggled with love as its giver, its receiver, and as love's gift itself.

I thank my children, and the men and women who have taught me how to love, by both loving me and allowing me to love them.

To you, the women I have loved in my life—thank you for allowing me to learn how you needed to love and how you needed to be loved. I have always looked upon each relationship as an invitation for me to learn another dimension of myself, a different me called forth by you.

I have not been an easy man to love. My own fears, my skepticism, and my primitive expectation that I will never be good enough for someone to stay—all haunted me periodically in my life. My eagerness to correct things and my impulse to fight earned me a lot of hatred from those I loved. But I always accepted struggle as part of the dance of learning about one another, learning how to live together, how to separate the ghosts of the past from the anxieties of the present.

To you, the men I have loved, my fathers, my brothers, my friends, my sons, I thank you for being there for me. Sadly, our love for one another was largely an unspoken one, more often an invitation to do something together, occasionally a teacher to a student. We loved through work and through play. We allowed our presence to say what we could not speak, and what our hearts hesitated to acknowledge. In death we can safely say it, without fear of ridicule or misinterpretation: I loved you, and I know you loved me.

Throughout my life, there have been two pieces of wisdom that have been central in my struggle to learn how to be a loving man. They are attributed to a man, Jesus of Nazareth, who in his life also struggled with the delicate balance between our impulse for justice and our higher calling to love one another.

The first is: "From him who has much, much will be asked." Since childhood I have viewed my life as an unending and cumulative learning experience. Everything— everything!—that I have learned has always been both fascinating at the time of my learning it, and a preparation for the next moment of my life wherein I would use that learned experience. With this philosophy of "Life-as-expanding-wisdom," I knew that I would have much to offer—and much to answer for.

And what would I use this knowledge data base for? To be heroic? To become famous? To compete with others? To be bragged about as wonderful, gifted, or outstanding? At different times in my life I'm sure I flirted with each of these ego trips. But the real secret was discerned most accurately by my family, who dubbed me, "Mr. Fix It." They knew that my passion was to discover in every context of life how to make it work—and work better than it did before. From light switches to fishing reels, from broken chairs to broken hearts, from family chaos to family fun. My obsession was not with what's wrong: my obsession was with how to make it right.

Which brings me to the second piece of guiding wisdom in my life. Again the words of Jesus:

"I have come that you might have life, and have it more abundantly."

What a powerful model he was in my life! What an invitation on which to focus! If my life had any meaning or purpose at all, then surely it contained the theme of so living my life, that *your* life be in some way enhanced by my presence. And if your life was diminished by my presence, then my life was not meant to be lived near you. This reality had been my motivation to "make it work," wherever I was. This theme urged me to promote the success and well-being of my family and friends. It was central to my work. It was the barometer of how I assessed my day: did my life add anything to the people whose lives I have touched? And when I failed to make my campsite better than how I found it, I wanted to know why. I wanted to learn how to do it differently the next time; and perhaps different will be better.

Don't get me wrong. I never believed that your happiness depended on my effort, nor that your unhappiness was caused by my failures. Either of these would have been sins of arrogance on my part. I have always believed that each of us is responsible for our well-being, and I have believed that we cannot and ought not to strive for this by ourselves, alone. Life is too short, too random, too imperfect, too frustrating for any of us not to make good use of our family and friends.

I have been there for you; you have been there for me. Without this, it all has no meaning, except as selfish and isolating death. This has been my learning about love.

That is why you are here today:

- to ask whether or not I have given according to all that was given me

- to assess whether my presence in your life through either my successes or failures moved you to a more abundant life
- to celebrate not just my life but yours because of what we shared
- to honor life that never ends
- to laugh together at me, at ourselves, and at all we do to prevent ourselves from loving one another

And though you feel some sadness that anchors your heart and rides on the waves of your laughter, remember this:

I am no longer there with you, but you are already here with me.

Amen.


*Afterthought*    So. How do we want to be remembered as men?

How will we wish we had lived our lives?

How will we wish we had lived this day?

# Conclusion

"Men *are* no damn good" is true when said with a smile, when spoken with humor, and when felt with love. When taken seriously, the expression is both an unfair and demeaning accusation as well as an excuse for the multiple childish and adolescent behaviors we men perpetuate throughout our lives.

Why is it so difficult for men to grow up? Why is it so difficult for women to expect their sons and husbands and brothers and fathers to eventually put away the things of a child and to put on the mantle of adulthood? Are men and women locked in a dance wherein neither is willing to let go of childhood, neither is courageous enough to move on to the less dramatic but more fulfilling diet of adult-to-adult companionship?

We're not talking about blaming or faulting here. We are simply raising the question of whether or not we even raise the question of how we prefer to be living our lives, not according to some unachievable ideal but according to our human potential. To use a well-worn expression: I think we have only just begun.

Perhaps some of our fear and confusion as men is the result of one of our finest qualities—our severe ability to categorize. It's either childhood or adulthood, following or leading, being good or being bad, sloppy or neat, uncaring or responsible, "with me or against me." Lighten up, guys! The real world of living adult males is not about either A or B, but about both A *and* B.

We don't have to leave the past behind: we carry the past with us. It enriches our current thoughts and feelings; it re-teaches and it informs our current decisions. The playful, risk-taking, even obnoxious parts of me live on in the context of my adult life of initiative, responsibility, and expansive love. Every day is an opportunity to update, revise, re-think, and re-experience my cumulative past, which, by the way, is what I call my Self.

We cripple ourselves when we take our image seriously. Those two words—"image" and "serious"—are the challenge of our future. How I think I have to look gets in the way of losing my self in a task or an exchange with someone I love. How seriously I assume I must be gets in the way of laughing at the utterly human life I am living. People can admire our image; no one can get close to us because of it. People can learn from our seriousness, they can fear us for our seriousness but they can't hug us or play with us or feel safe in our cool seriousness.

Manhood is not about assuming a serious, correct posture in life. That's what a knight does when he dons his suit of armor. He must be helped onto his horse, handed his jousting pole, and is so laden with the weight and balance of it all that he is knocked off by the slightest jolt. He sits in the dust, stunned, and thinks to himself, "I'm not having any fun."

Manhood is rather like throwing a ball back and forth with someone you like. It's about testing your windup, aiming for a target, teasing the catcher, hurling your best shot, and laughing till it hurts when you miss by a mile. Manhood is about your throws being your own. Manhood is about making the exchange interesting for your partner. Manhood is creating a dynamic balance between *what* you're doing and doing it *together*.

Every partner we choose creates a different game of catch. Play to win, and we lose a partner. Play to lose, and our partner loses us. Play seriously, and we lose the game. Play cautiously, and we lose the play.

So let's at least raise the questions. How am I moving through my life? How do I want to be remembered? What example do I wish to be for those who follow me? Has my life mattered?

Then we die. And suddenly we are standing before the Big Gate in The Sky and St. Peter calls us by name. We individually step forward, and with a warm smile, he asks us a single question:

"Sir, did you have a good time?"

Panic! He didn't ask if we were good or bad. He didn't ask what we accomplished, how many toys we accumulated, what we've built, what changes we made, what battles we won, what religion we practiced, what books we wrote, what awards we received. We were ready for those questions. But he didn't ask a single one. Instead, he wants to know if we enjoyed the trip, for God's sake!

There it is, fellas. What will your answer be? There will be no lying this time. And I warn you. Should your answer be, "No, Mr. Peter, I guess I didn't, not really," then know in advance, he will respond:

"Well, now, I'm sorry to hear that. We're gonna have to send you back to re-read *Men Are No Damn Good!*"

Eugene J. Webb